More than bits of idle magic,

they showed the world the heart of God.

THE MIRACLES OF CHRIST

All of Christ's miracles are spectacular, instantaneous, visible thrills but the astounding wonder is the way they always go hand in hand with His good deeds, like a legible crown to His compassion. The devil himself can do wonders; Jesus will not do them except to echo heaven. A New Testament miracle is physical evidence of a spiritual explosion, a personal note in God's own handwriting, written in flesh and blood to a particular address. Each of them announces and rehearses in miniature the day when heaven and earth will come together as the rule instead of the exception.

—From the book

HARPER JUBILEE BOOKS

THE
MIRACLES
OF
CHRIST

David A. Redding

HARPER & ROW, PUBLISHERS
New York, Hagerstown, San Francisco, London

To my
father and mother
and my little sister

and

To my mother and father—
by marriage—
DR. AND MRS. JOHN MAXWELL MCCLEERY

THE MIRACLES OF CHRIST

PREFACE

The modern world generally objects to the miracles of Christ. Those "mighty works" that used to make so much sense and so many friends now make more work, much confusion, and many higher critics. Spinoza declares emphatically that miracles are impossible, Hume claims that they are incredible, and Schleiermacher insists that they are only harmlessly relative. They have made many suspicious that Christ's miracles were made up out of the blind enthusiasm of apostolic promotion.

The church's pride and joy has become her problem child and Scripture's muscle has become embarrassing. Ministers are kept busy brushing unwelcome wonders out of touchy long hair or are taught to explain them away deftly if they get in the way of the Scripture lesson. Scholars salvage symbolic odds and ends from the decay of belief as preachers pick their way through the theological debris for any scrap of data that can be substantiated by modern psychology. Before thinking men give in to the prevailing winds of the present cold academic climate and surrender Christ's miracles wholesale, they had better try to decide why Someone put them there in the Scriptures.

Mankind shows no sign of having outgrown miracles; men have merely exchanged Christ's miracles for those of Edison and Einstein. Even such a skeptic as George Bernard Shaw believed that the typical college graduate is guilty of far more blind faith than all our forefathers in the Dark Ages. Shaw insisted that it is naive to think we are less naive than Joan of Arc:

> The medieval doctors of divinity who did not pretend to settle how many angels could dance on the point of a needle cut a very poor figure as far as romantic credulity is concerned beside the modern physicists who have settled to the billionth of a millimetre every movement and position in the dance of the elec-

trons. Not for worlds would I question the precise accuracy of these calculations or the existence of electrons (whatever they may be). The fate of Joan is a warning to me against such heresy. But why the men who believe in electrons should regard themselves as less credulous than the men who believed in angels is not apparent to me.

Before we can view the towering faith of our fathers fairly, we must notice how far our faith has gone on in physics. The secular faith that flourishes under our noses now, fitting us so snugly that we never notice how fantastic it is, will surely bring smiles to the lips of our children tomorrow—or tears to their eyes. Before we end up in Aldous Huxley's unbowed and bloodless *Brave New World* (which will eliminate miracles and dismiss God to make everything lifelessly efficient and desolately self-sufficient)—before we cross out Christ and snip His most thrilling moments from our minds while we bargain for a future that looks less and less inviting because He is not invited—we might weigh these words by the writer of *Saint Joan*:

As to the new rites, which would be the saner Joan? The one who carried little children to be baptized of water and the spirit, or the one who sent the police to force their parents to have the most villainous racial poison we know thrust into their veins? The one who told them the story of the angel and Mary, or the one who questioned them as to their experiences of the Edipus complex? The one to whom the consecrated wafer was the very body of the virtue that was her salvation, or the one who looked forward to a precise and convenient regulation of her health and her desires by a nicely calculated diet of thyroid extract, adrenalin, thymin, pituitrin, and insulin, with pick-me-ups of hormone stimulants, the blood being first carefully fortified with antibodies against all possible infections by innoculations of infected bacteria and serum from infected animals, and against old age by surgical extirpation of the reproductive ducts or weekly doses of monkey gland.

We must not allow Shaw to smear the long strides science has heroically made in the twentieth century in the conquest of hardship and disease. But perhaps our age has been fruitlessly preoccupied with technicalities. Surely it is not reactionary to pray that the day of experts may recapture a mood of wonder and an apostolic sense of proportion and divine purpose—a happier synthesis. Our narrow specialization suffers in meaningless sterility unless the Spirit blends it in on the larger canvas.

After all, the chief requirement for learning truth in any time is humility. Paul learned much from ignorant fishermen, and the great Tolstoy finally turned to peasants for the answer he sought. So we, the specialists of the Space Age, ought to take another look at this old Book as men who have not arrived and who do not have all the answers, remembering how He said, "Except ye . . . become as little children, ye shall not enter into the kingdom of heaven."

We cannot come to the miracles of Christ until we come to the miracle of Christ Himself. Christ's miracles seem ridiculous to anyone who cannot believe that Christ is miraculous. If God is the "Father Almighty" and Jesus is "His only Son, our Lord," then we have at least made room for His miracles. We could, of course, completely spiritualize the miracles or shrink them into symbols but that would squeeze the dynamic New Testament life out of them. These miracles are meaningless except in the context of faith in the Miracle Worker. Nobody but disciples ever saw the risen Christ; nobody but believers will ever be prepared to believe that He could do the impossible.

"And this being so," as Archbishop Trench tried to tell us a long time ago, "we should learn betimes how futile it is to argue with men about *our* faith who are the deniers of all upon which *any* faith can be built." Christ's miracles are not our propaganda pills for pagans. Unbelievers could never swallow them, for, as Fyodor Dostoevsky has said, "Faith does not, in the realist, spring from the miracles, but the miracles from faith."

Christ Himself is so magnificent to His followers—such a shining Star of light and sacrifice, so bright a Slave of need, and such a mighty Arm of God—that they can never begin to find words high enough to reach up and do Him justice. His disciples know only that He cannot be neatly put down in black and white; He is too big, too illusive, to fit into any cockpit of finite definition. And so, for those who find that they can call Him Lord and Master, any miracles He does seem minor beside the blazing wonder of who He is. The unbelievable wonder to those who believe is that Someone so divine should have done nothing out of the ordinary.

The great miracle is the incarnation; all else, so to speak, follows naturally and of course. And as he believes that greatest miracle, so will he believe all other miracles, which, as satellites of a lesser brightness, naturally wait on and cluster round and draw their lustre from the central brightness of that one. So that it may more truly be said that we believe the miracles for Christ's sake, than Christ for the miracles' sake.

What does the word "miracle" mean? In a way, the whole world itself is a miracle; so is every word, every baby's birth, all life, and our next breath. But this study is fascinated by the thirty-five miracles, more or less, that the New Testament tells us Jesus did. How do we distinguish these specific miracles from all the other miracles God does in general?

"What we commonly call miracles are, in the sacred Scriptures, termed sometimes 'wonders' ($\tau\acute{\epsilon}\rho\alpha\tau\alpha$), sometimes 'signs' ($\sigma\eta\mu\epsilon\hat{\iota}\alpha$), sometimes 'powers' ($\delta\upsilon\nu\acute{\alpha}\mu\epsilon\iota\varsigma$), sometimes simply 'works' ($\acute{\epsilon}\rho\gamma\alpha$)." It is very significant that in the New Testament the word "wonder" is never written alone but always with the words "signs" or "powers." Christ's miracles are not isolated bits of idle magic to show Him off; they are always answers to prayer. They are stunning illustrations in real life which flower from faith in the life-giving finger of God.

All of Christ's miracles are spectacular, instantaneous, visible thrills but the astounding wonder is the way they always go hand in hand with His good deeds, like a legible crown to His compassion. The devil himself can do wonders; Jesus will not do them except to echo heaven. A New Testament miracle is physical evidence of a spiritual explosion, a personal note in God's own handwriting, written in flesh and blood to a particular address. Each of them announces and rehearses in miniature the day when heaven and earth will come together as the rule instead of the exception.

The sharpest question stabbing the very idea of miracles today is simply, Do miracles break the laws of nature? No. "We say," said Augustine ages ago, "that all portents [miracles] are contrary to nature, but they are not so. For how is that contrary to nature which happens by the will of God, since the will of so mighty a Creator is certainly the nature of each created thing? A portent therefore happens not contrary to nature, but contrary to what we know as nature."

Archbishop Trench adds, "We should term the miracle not the infraction of law, but behold in it the lower law neutralized, and for the time put out of working by a higher. . . . Thus, when I lift my arm, the law of gravitation is not, as far as my arm is concerned, denied or annihilated; it exists as much as ever, but is held in suspense by the higher law of my will." The Great Physician who has all the laws, known and unknown to us, at His beck and call can do whatever extraordinary things He wills to do within the structure of scientific law.

We do not live under a reign of law; God reigns and He is not imprisoned by His own house rules. The earth does work like a vast machine, but the Maker runs it and can make it do anything He wants. He is God, not a figurehead. Laws are not His limitations, His abdication; they are the tools of the divine Maintenance and Repairman. And as in darkest Africa some natives could never understand how a missionary was saved from the deadly bite of a witch doctor's spider by the miracle of a magnifying glass which "burned," so we stand in awe before the more stupefying miracles of the One who is our Master.

We will not come to unanimous agreement before such a miracle as the miracles of Christ. But if He is our Lord and Master, our Maker's only Son, He will do some things "far beyond our poor power to add or detract." If everything in our New Testament were as plain as day and as easily mastered as third-grade arithmetic, we would have good reason to think we had outgrown it. The fact that there are a few things left in our faith beyond the grasp of finite mind gives us reason to believe it is the Word of God.

Today we find the world poised on the razor's edge. Our pain-killers have brought us no peace, but we have new addicts; many of the best men still go out of their minds and more die in shallow sanity. We have developed the perfect suicide pill for the whole planet, and when one man decides to take it he will take the rest of mankind with him. The only prerogative left to the great powers is the dubious honor of being the first to administer the potion.

We have reasoned ourselves into a corner and the only way out is up. We have fought ourselves to a stalemate. God-hungry men, sitting in their chrome cages of futility, beg to ask the question John the Baptist sent from his dungeon cell almost two thousand years ago: "Are you the one who is to come, or are we to expect some other?" From across the years the answer comes back to anyone who cares to listen: " 'Go,' he said, 'and tell John what you have seen and heard: how the blind recover their sight, the lame walk, the lepers are clean, the deaf hear, the dead are raised to life, the poor are hearing the good news—and happy is the man who does not find me a stumbling-block.' "

David A. Redding

ACKNOWLEDGMENTS

Next to the Miracle Worker Himself and the four men who gave us the primary sources in the New Testament, the man to whom I am most indebted is a nineteenth-century Englishman named Richard C. Trench, whose *Notes on the Miracles of Our Lord* still stands as the most comprehensive authority in the field. That notable work was written from the rare perspective of a man who was both a great scholar of Christ's miracles and a deep believer in them. Secondly, I want to pay especial tribute to the distinguished contributors, particularly to Volumes VII and VIII, of *The Interpreter's Bible* for the mass of research and scholarship they made so readily available to me.

Particular thanks is due to Frances Cronise Weaver, my secretary, for her excellent assistance in typing and preparing the manuscript for publication, and for the gracious and competent job of editing done by Phyllis Murphy. I am also deeply grateful for the good counsel and helpful suggestions I received from my able friends: Helen Loos Whitney, Duris Woods Cary, Dr. Charles C. Patterson, the Reverend M. William Glandon, and Dr. John Maxwell McCleery. It is difficult to measure the huge contribution of my wife, Dorothy McCleery Redding, and the vast patience and moral support I have received from my congregation. And lastly, let me say that I am much obliged to you, my reader.

And chiefly Thou, O Spirit, that dost prefer
Before all temples the upright heart and pure,
Instruct me, for Thou know'st; . . .
    What in me is dark
Illumine, what is low raise and support;
That, to the highth of this great argument,
I may assert Eternal Providence,
And justify the ways of God to men.

—JOHN MILTON, *Paradise Lost*

THE MIRACLES OF CHRIST

CONTENTS

THE MIRACLES OF CHRIST

·I·

The
Mastery
of Nature

CHAPTER 1

And the third day there was a marriage in Cana of Galilee; and the mother of Jesus was there: And both Jesus was called, and his disciples, to the marriage. And when they wanted wine, the mother of Jesus saith unto him, They have no wine. Jesus saith unto her, Woman, what have I to do with thee? mine hour is not yet come. His mother saith unto the servants, Whatsoever he saith unto you, do it. And there were set there six waterpots of stone, after the manner of the purifying of the Jews, containing two or three firkins apiece. Jesus saith unto them, Fill the waterpots with water. And they filled them up to the brim. And he saith unto them, Draw out now, and bear unto the governor of the feast. And they bare it. When the ruler of the feast had tasted the water that was made wine, and knew not whence it was: (but the servants which drew the water knew;) the governor of the feast called the bridegroom, And saith unto him, Every man at the beginning doth set forth good wine; and when men have well drunk, then that which is worse: but thou hast kept the good wine until now. This beginning of miracles did Jesus in Cana of Galilee, and manifested forth his glory; and his disciples believed on him.

JOHN 2:1-11, KING JAMES VERSION

Turning Water Into Wine

IF WE WANT to meet this miracle we must treat it as a masterpiece to love, not as an hypothesis to shoot full of holes. Sometimes we are so suspicious that Scripture will fool us that we are afraid to sit back and enjoy it. We are so terrified of what scholarship will say that we don't dare let God take our breath away. But let us sit down now, defenselessly, as if for the first time, at the foot of this sketch the favorite wrote of his Master. If God will let Christ do a miracle here, why should we try to stop Him? The least we can do is give it the courtesy of our attention, and the most that can happen to us is that we might get "lost in wonder, love, and praise."

"This beginning of miracles did Jesus in Cana of Galilee. . . ." The Miracle Worker's first attempt would make an unforgettable impression. He did not know His own strength; so where would He go—what mountain would be high enough?—to try out "the power and the glory" for the first time? We could never guess that He would fling away His first miracle as a lighthearted bouquet to romantic love and friendly laughter in the middle of a noisy wedding party.

We can imagine a modern promotion agent begging Jesus to begin with a spectacular healing at a leper colony. We can hear some killjoy shouting, "Your career will never recover from such a scandal as working with wine at a wedding reception! You ought to go to grief first, or to church—

religion can always play safe there. Old heads will shake with shock if God's pure power is poured out not on a few select Pharisees fasting soberly but showered intemperately and promiscuously on a rowdy reception. John the Baptist would never dream of doing such a thing! He never went to weddings, anyway, and he would disappear into the desert to do justice to such an occasion as this."

However, the disciple whom Jesus loved made a point of presenting his Master in the midst of merriment. Jesus did not need a protected, monastic setting to display His power; He went where life was and hallowed any scene. He was never out of place. Jesus' best friend did his best in this preliminary scene to prevent Jesus from ever being unfairly billed as a drab and deadly martyr who, without His cross, would be a wallflower anywhere. On the contrary, this early glimpse at Cana shows Christ most completely at home in mixed company and loving life for all its worth.

We cannot forget the day Christ's anger mounted in the Temple, nor the days that drew tears, and the nights spent in prayer. He lived a full life; and when the time came, He knew how to make a sacrifice. But John first fixes our attention on something dreary Christians have covered up: the happy Christ who knew how to laugh and could show us all how to have a good time. The cross and the Bible are so noticeable in the contemporary chancel that we fail to see that both are still supported by the banquet table. Perhaps the overreaction of our prevalent guilt complex to His rebukes robs our recollection of the time when the neighbors complained about Him for not fasting as John and his disciples did, and for behaving like "a gluttonous man, and winebibber." The black robes of the clergy and the black cover of the Bible do not completely represent the Christ who referred to Himself as a Bridegroom and to His group of friends as a bridal party. The glum paintings of Him that most of us remember have almost eliminated John's description of the light side of the Master. That sunny day in Cana heralds the bright story of one condemned Man whose last meal was festive with hope, who in the shadow of His cross turned the conversation to "my joy." He once introduced God's Kingdom as buried treasure; He insisted that the shepherd's reaction to the lost sheep was not punitive but joyful; and He was known to illustrate the last judgment with a story of a bridegroom returning for a housewarming.

Lest anyone think that this miracle at Cana gives him license to splurge in alcohol, it ought to be clear that the dominant feature of that feast was Christ's presence. Anyone who has ever gone where men are trying to live it up without a blessing knows what a pitiful effort it is. It goes without saying that grief needs God's help; gladness needs it, too. The *good* time that tries to get away with something, to have fun at the expense of fair play and thoughtfulness, never quite comes off. The night out from God—as if we could get along all right without Him—is a crude contradiction.

John was trying to make clear what the cheater in us wants to forget—that Christ alone is the life of the party. Without God right beside them the human side of men dies and they indulge in a repetition of the same old orgy of coarse animal spirits, reverting to their usual weaknesses and faults the same way they regretted the last time they are still trying to forget. Conversation becomes loud and dull, harder and heavier-handed, cheaper, until finally some souls are put to sleep, and some go to the dogs, and the discussion descends. How ugly the wedding reception becomes without Him! What a miracle He brings to it!

". . . and the mother of Jesus was there." It is exciting to find the first lady here, for she usually stays silently by the crêche or the cross in our memories. This is her first appearance in John's gospel. To her, the occasion must have seemed her Son's send-off, her farewell. In that touching scene-behind-the-scene the young widow gave her Son away to God. We know what was immediately ahead of Him, but she was His mother and had pondered an aching heartful of that future. Artists have had a hard time painting the Man; the mother is not an easy subject, either. She lived with Him longest, under the sweet spell of His birth, His boy's life, and through the shattering adolescence of divinity. Gabriel had made his speech to her. What growing pains, what powers had she seen as she watched Him grow up out of her arms and into Godhood? She must have alternately sunk with foreboding, then sucked in her breath for joy, as she saw the cross's shadow streaming down in the starlight. If wise men could not believe He was simply Joseph's boy—and if all the saints, after it was all over, sensed that something unbelievably sacred must have passed between Mary and God—what virgin secret did this woman keep that she could bear the world its Prince?

She seemed to be a close friend of the family giving the feast, for she came to the rescue in neighborly solicitude when the refreshment ran out. That she cared about so domestic a crisis says something, and that she had confidence in her Son tells more. She had scolded Jesus as a Boy for staying too late at the temple, and later on she seemed to question His good sense when she stood outside where He was preaching and tried to get Him to come home. This picture catches her introducing Him to society in easy confidence and motherly partiality: "Do whatever he tells you." Jesus' answer sounds cross in English but the Greek form of the address is tender and intimate, as if to say, "Never mind, don't be worried." They speak to each other as if she had learned long ago to worship the ground He walked upon and He had learned how to look after her.

The story also suggests her sending Him out to help us. Mothers usually rear their sons to be successful; Mary intended hers to wait on others in most menial service. So John announces Him to the world doing domestic work, as if He were doing the dishes because His mother told Him to do them. Jesus did not exploit His qualifications to compete for plums. He decided to do the things other men felt were beneath them. He did, not what they couldn't do, but wouldn't do. Taking plenty of time to please God, He assisted a poverty-stricken father of a bride or groom to be a generous host. As Dostoevsky declared: "Of course, they were poor, since they hadn't wine enough even at a wedding. . . . The historians write that, in those days, the people living about the lake of Gennesaret were the poorest that can possibly be imagined."

"Now six stone jars were standing there, for the Jewish rites of purification, each holding twenty or thirty gallons." John takes every precaution to cut off any other possible conclusion except miracle. He starts out with six empty water jars and forces the reader to watch as the full amount of water is poured in each jar. The groundwork for the miracle is prepared so deliberately and unmistakably that there is no way out of belief except outright distrust of John or Jesus.

Is this asking too much of the modern mind? Surely it was even harder for the ancient mind. Our great-grandfathers were not the simpletons our fathers often thought they were, and they didn't have the benefit of our educational marvels. Is it asking too much of any mind to believe that "The conscious water saw its God and blushed"?

No miracle can be simple and still be a miracle. Miracles are not for fools and they astound the superior by the supreme. Christ would not turn stones into bread to show off for Satan or to save Himself; yet, shortly after, He turned water into wine to help a poor man put on a wedding feast. But He did no violence to nature. God makes grape juice out of rainwater annually, although at Cana it was remarkably accelerated and completely independent of any vineyard or hired hands.

Do we have to deny authority to Jesus in dimensions we

don't know anything about? After all, our magicians, our chemists, and our surgeons can do even better things, and while the amateur eye cannot keep up with them, we know there is a logical explanation. Should we limit God to less than we allow to men, especially when He had so good a reason to gladden the poor and to give Christ glory?

Since the miracle was already recorded in Scripture before we got here, and our judgment about its being included in the canon was not solicited, we cannot get rid of it. We have to run the risk of either too much faith or too little. But why does a man doubt this miracle? Intelligence? But brilliant men have believed it, and I believe that unbelief betrays a bigger reason than reason. Our unbelief, despite the loud protests, declares a lack of confidence in Christ's ability and the Bible's dependability. Anyone who eliminates a miracle here and there does not display a talent for exegesis so much as a lack of enthusiasm. The joker is that our mental reservations excuse—in fact, encourage—a cool and distant discipleship. If we accept the gospels as truth they will overpower us and we will have no reluctant leg to stand on. But if we can keep thinking up questions we can stall for more time instead of giving Him the rare courtesy of prompt and unconditional surrender.

The miracle of turning water into wine is a test case for every Christian. In a way it is the most difficult miracle of them all, but we cannot discard it. We cannot stand aside from Scripture to judge whether a particular paragraph is acceptable, as if we were too good or too smart for it. That has all been decided; now it is there to judge us. The strictly scholarly slant lets in the door an approach that swiftly obliterates the final authority of Scripture as the Word of God. If we can reject this miracle, then we are free to pick at the rest, and souvenir hunters soon make short work of the Old, Old Story. If we read the Bible for critical reasons, instead of trying to see what the Holy Spirit has to say to us, some other less valid criterion than the canon soon insinuates itself and dogmatically supersedes it as our "only infallible rule." When we read to master the text, rather than to be mastered by it, we shift the control of the situation from the script to the commentary, or to our own faculties, and we are then at the whim of the times or whatever passion happens to be sweeping over us at the moment. Our verdict of any piece of Holy Writ is inconsequential compared to its comment to us. It has—and long after we are dead and gone it will still have—the last word.

I think the best we can do with any portion of prophecy that lies beyond the eye of faith is to pray, "Lord, I believe; help Thou my unbelief." That is also the least we can do as long as we live as those under authority.

". . . the water . . . become wine. . . ." The scene at Cana is not a pitch for the host of distinction. It distills a deeper truth. Jesus' performance that day is far above the field of fermentation. It is John's way of showing His mastery of spiritual alchemy. This Man can put eternal fire into the veins of dying men. It is popular to dismiss Christianity as a "hands-off" policy where the answer is always "no." "God," the truants keep telling each other, "is frightfully strict and looks suspiciously like grim Grandfather Calvin." But there was nothing negative about Christ at Cana and that positive step paced His way to the cross. His presence was intoxicating, sobering —the very thing prescribed for us. Given a crust, He prepares a banquet fit for a king. Granted a few loaves and fishes, He revives five thousand people. Everything He touches turns under His green thumb—the water to wine, the grave to resurrection.

"Jesus said to them, 'Fill the jars with water.' And they filled them up to the brim. He said to them, 'Now draw some out, and take it to the steward of the feast.' So they took it."

Jesus did not move in like a magician, requesting everyone to stand back so that He could make a grandstand play. He took the waiters into the miracle with Him and kept it from the crowd.

Jesus was not after credit. Time after time He told the rescued not to mention His name, and down through the years of Christian service He has quietly erased His fingerprints on goodness. Who here could deny that he has had some help from Him, but who could tell exactly how or when it was? He and the One who made us do not point to Themselves. God does not answer prayer with fanfare, nor does He publicly disclaim the blame He gets for the devil's work.

As much as the story at Cana may seem an affront to someone's intelligence, it never assaults our sense of modesty. Christ worked so invisibly that even the steward complimented the bridegroom: "When the steward of the feast tasted the water now become wine, . . . [he] called the bridegroom and said to him, 'Every man serves the good wine first; and when men have drunk freely, then the poor wine; but you have kept the good wine until now.'" Life sours for so many people before they can finish it; the last drink is acid and the last drop death. So men stir fitfully and gulp frantically at the first years. Hollywood tips us off to the thrills at the front of life—Take another trip through romance while you can!—This is it!

Christ Himself is the magic ingredient that makes life improve with age. The disciple whom Jesus loved wrote from experience near the end of his life, reaffirming that God actually saves the good wine till last—"which ye shall one day drink with Me new in the Kingdom of God." Our day in Cana melts away in a rich sunset of color and we see the steward twisting his glass in a bewilderment of joy. "This beginning of miracles did Jesus in Galilee, and manifested forth his glory; and his disciples believed on him."

CHAPTER 2

Some time later Jesus withdrew to the farther shore of the Sea of Galilee (or Tiberias), and a large crowd of people followed who had seen the signs he performed in healing the sick. Then Jesus went up the hill-side and sat down with his disciples. It was near the time of Passover, the great Jewish festival. Raising his eyes and seeing a large crowd coming towards him, Jesus said to Philip, 'Where are we to buy bread to feed these people?' This he said to test him; Jesus himself knew what he meant to do. Philip replied, 'Twenty pounds would not buy enough bread for every one of them to have a little.' One of his disciples, Andrew, the brother of Simon Peter, said to him, 'There is a boy here who has five barley loaves and two fishes; but what is that among so many?' Jesus said, 'Make the people sit down.' There was plenty of grass there, so the men sat down, about five thousand of them. Then Jesus took the loaves, gave thanks, and distributed them to the people as they sat there. He did the same with the fishes, and they had as much as they wanted. When everyone had had enough, he said to his disciples, 'Collect the pieces left over, so that nothing may be lost.' This they did, and filled twelve baskets with the pieces left uneaten of the five barley loaves. When the people saw the sign Jesus had performed, the word went round, 'Surely this must be the prophet that was to come into the world.' Jesus, aware that they meant to come and seize him to proclaim him king, withdrew again to the hills by himself.

JOHN 6:1-15 (ALSO MATTHEW 14:15-21; MARK 6:35:-44; LUKE 9:12-17), NEW ENGLISH BIBLE

There was another occasion about this time when a huge crowd had collected, and, as they had no food, Jesus called his disciples and said to them, 'I feel sorry for all these people; they have been with me now for three days and have nothing to eat. If I send them home unfed, they will turn faint on the way; some of them have come from a distance.' The disciples answered, 'How can anyone provide all these people with bread in this lonely place?' 'How many loaves have you?' he asked; and they answered, 'Seven.' So he ordered the people to sit down on the ground; then he took the seven loaves, and, after giving thanks to God, he broke the bread and gave it to his disciples to distribute; and they served it out to the people. They had also a few small fishes, which he blessed and ordered them to distribute. They all ate to their hearts' content, and seven baskets were filled with the scraps that were left. The people numbered about four thousand. Then he dismissed them; and, without delay, got into the boat with his disciples and went to the district of Dalmanutha.

MARK 8:1-10 (ALSO MATTHEW 15:32-39), NEW ENGLISH BIBLE

Feeding the Five Thousand
Feeding the Four Thousand

THE FEEDING OF the five thousand is the only one of Christ's miracles that got into all four gospels. Apparently that day made such a deep impression that no one could forget it. Few incidents, even in Scripture, come to us with such good credentials, and each writer offers us his favorite details.

It was such a breathtakingly beautiful day out there near Bethsaida by the sea. The grass was green, Mark said, where they all sat down, and they had their own mountain next door to crown the view. The setting is still perfect for a miracle— if we can find some faith to go with it.

What was everybody doing on that hillside in the first place? The gospels give us several good reasons. Mark mentions that the seventy had just reported back, mission completed. Jesus saw how much they deserved some peace and quiet, and thoughtfully recommended a retreat.

"For many were coming and going, and they had no leisure even to eat." All of the writers also remember that the event took place hard on the heels of John the Baptist's death, and Matthew especially senses the shock and anguish the heart-breaking news brought to Christ. And so, in his gospel, when Jesus hears that the brave and beloved Baptist was beheaded we read these tear-filled words: "Now when Jesus heard this, he withdrew from there in a boat to a lonely place apart." They all had had enough. It was time to go where they would not be bothered.

But Jesus didn't get His way. Life's humor and hard times are always mixed up, and God gave the little band a good laugh first: "Now many saw them going, . . . and ran there on foot . . . and got there ahead of them." The Great Physician was no sooner in the boat than He saw His patients mobbing His vacation spot. Imagine an overworked doctor's reaction if he found patients lining the driveway of his summer place! Jesus and His friends, out in their boat, watched helplessly while rushing crowds defeated the purpose of their trip. Any hopes for sleep went up in the dust raised by thousands of feet along the shore.

How did Jesus take it? It must have struck Him as one of the most humorous things that ever happened to Him, but His faith kept Him flexible: "As he landed he saw a great throng, and he had compassion on them, because they were like sheep without a shepherd; and he began to teach them . . . ," "and healed their sick." His good humor at that moment was even more of a miracle than the one we're coming to. Jesus saw that others also were suffering from the death of John. It was time for the Passover and Jesus knew that the accumulating pilgrims were missing their old shepherd more than ever.

Jesus' disciples took it as long as they could but when it grew late and they saw that the crowd would make short work of their supper they came to the conclusion that the crowd would have to go. So they came to Jesus with advice: "This is a lonely place, and the hour is now late; send them away, to go into the country and villages round about and buy themselves something to eat."

The situation was hopeless to the disciples and they had given up. But Jesus did not know how to throw up His hands.

"You give them something to eat." He never quarreled with circumstances and never dumped anything that was dropped in His lap. He believed that problems were meant to be solved, not refused, and that the answers would soon come along. God is always in the picture somewhere, coming to the rescue, if we will sit tight and stay alert. Nothing is too far beyond or beneath God, and the very things that are too big for us are ready-made for God to do.

Jesus showed us how to live in subordination to God's will. Our place is not to call the shots but to follow up. ". . . all things work together for good to them that love God . . . ," and each predicament is an education in God's skill. Man's worst disaster gives God the best chance to demonstrate omnipotence. Christ had faith that the end of the world would mean the beginning of a better one.

Three gospels give the disciples away for worrying about eating arrangements but John said Jesus asked Philip first: "Where are we to buy bread to feed these people?" Why did Jesus pick Philip? John confided that Jesus already knew what He was going to do and questioned Philip only to test him. Apparently, Philip's spiritual thickness at times put even Thomas to shame. Christ could hardly believe His ears when Philip asked something elementary at the last minute— "Philip, have you been so long with Me and yet not known?" Jesus was trying to get through to Philip on this occasion, to see whether Philip could figure out a dilemma through faith instead of shrugging it off as if it should never have happened. Perhaps He hoped to hear Philip say, "Lord, You can get us through this; You will think of something." Instead, Philip believed the problem was bigger than both of them and backed down. "Twenty pounds," he cried, naming a sum beyond their means yet far short of the solution. "Twenty pounds would not buy enough bread for every one of them to have a little."

Jesus realized that men have stomachs as well as souls. Many have complained about the way in which Jesus fed the five thousand; but they would have been harder on Him if He hadn't cared whether or not they went to bed hungry. We must not let His divine manners hide His warm hospitality. As confusing as this miracle may be, it brings Jesus down to earth where we are. Here is a Man who likes to see men eat and wouldn't let them leave until everyone had had supper. This miracle is not the meaningless entertainment of a strong man foolishly flexing his muscle. Christ's miracles reflect excellent taste—He knew exactly what people needed.

Jesus did not look down on the crowd, as if they were no better than a mob, and give them a lecture on "the wrath to come." Instead, He gave them bread. They were no trouble at all and He was honored to have them as His personal guests.

Andrew did a little better than Philip. At least, he had looked around and taken inventory of the bare cupboard and he had the nerve to mention something so microscopic that the other disciples must have laughed it off. There they were in the middle of five thousand hungry, milling mouths and Andrew came out with: "There is a lad here who has five barley loaves and two fish. . . ." Since tension must have been mounting by the minute, that statement was the last straw. But Andrew risked those words to One who never made fun of someone else's confidence, and his scrap of faith was all Jesus needed. He took the start that Andrew gave Him and did something with it that afternoon; and to this day the whole world knows of Andrew's contribution.

The boy himself did not do badly. He did not hide his lunch somewhere under a rock. He must have been hungry, too, but he was generous. Some mother had packed a lunch that morning that would go down in history as the grandest dinner ever spread. Even millions of unbelievers would hear about it. There were five rolls, slightly larger than our bakers' buns, and two smoked fish. More incredible than Jesus' influence on the repast is the fact that after all these years we are still discussing the potential wealth that was packed in a boy's lunch box.

Jesus said, "Make them sit down in companies, about fifty each." That seems so simple; yet in all likelihood, had we been caught in that traffic jam we would never have thought of it, let alone had the power to execute it. It was an inspiration that immediately brought military order out of complete chaos. No doubt the green grass, the setting sun, and the quiet sea just giving birth to the Jordan, brought home the tranquillity of the place as the people were being seated.

"Jesus then took the loaves, and when he had given thanks, he distributed them. . . ; so also the fish. . . ." Thanks was no small thing with Him, as we can see. His banquets would not begin before grace. Apparently it pleased God for He saved His Son embarrassment by making up the difference. Jesus began with the little serving He had, with complete faith that God would add a giant helping. It worked! What more can a man say after God uses one of His superlatives?—except that our new electronic ovens and instant coffee have nothing on the One who built creation overnight.

"And when they had eaten their fill. . . ." This is no slick explanation and one marvels at the restraint the gospel writers exercised. No one makes it harder to believe by trying to make it easier. Jesus simply fed five thousand people out of a boy's lunch basket. Thank God, Scripture always leaves the unsayable unsaid. It makes an announcement to all ages, then leaves it to each age to fill in the details in its own way. The Bible doesn't care how Jesus did it or how God did it. It insists on one thing only—that men admit the miracle of God doing enough to make a man believe.

Imagine the controversies that would have developed if Scripture had gone into the science of creation, plotting meteors and pinpointing volcanoes, giving the exact time of day when China was carried in or Australia peeped through the surface of the Pacific. All those facts would be very absorbing, but in the end who cares "when" and "how"? Deep down in our hearts we ache to know "who" and "why". "In the beginning God . . ."—God is the Starmaker, the Sunmaker, the Rainmaker. He split the Red Sea and snowed manna on the heads of starving pilgrims in the wilderness. Scripture will not split hairs, nor answer impertinent questions as if it were on the witness stand trying to defend itself against the opposition. The Bible could have gone on to fill shelves with endless data and dates—when God added adenoids, what time in the afternoon of time He straightened man's back, which part first, and why He did it that way. The Book passes over the useless paraphernalia to tell us the one thing we need to know: God made man in His own image.

The disciples kept their noses out of God's pantry and asked no rude questions of their Host. They did not argue about how the bread bulged and the fishes flew as His fingers touched them. What God was wearing that day or the size of His vast larder is kept appropriately out of sight to save a little room for faith.

"When everyone had had enough, he said to his disciples, 'Collect the pieces left over, so that nothing may be lost.'" Each crumb of sacramental bread is more precious than the piece of wedding cake we saved. He would not desecrate the hill with litter, nor waste food, despite the bounty. But, between the lines, we read the lesson to the disciples who feared that their frugal meal would suddenly disappear into five thousand mouths. To their credit the disciples told this pettiness on themselves. They confessed frankly that they "filled twelve baskets with the pieces left uneaten of the five barley loaves"—one for each disciple, none for Christ. This line of the story shows up the absurdity of our ever being afraid to give for fear there won't be anything left for ourselves. God takes good care of His givers; we do not need to be afraid of the unexpected guest whom God invites.

After dinner, according to John, the crowd went wild trying to make Christ their king. The devil had already tried to do it and every age has always been able to think up a better description for Him. The crowd wanted Him to go into politics, while we want Him to stay out. Our day accuses Him of being impractical, while His own family suspected His sanity and tried to get Him to abandon His ministry and come home. Jesus decided, however, that the world did not need another Alexander as much as a Saviour; before they had time to crown Him, "Jesus withdrew again to the hills by himself." Some day men may be ready to admit that He knew what He was doing.

Actually this miracle didn't end until a few days later when Jesus had to correct a few stragglers who were still hanging on, trying to take advantage of His kitchen privileges. He saw through them immediately: ". . . you have come looking for me because your hunger was satisfied with the loaves you ate. . . ." But Jesus refused to be the victim of parasites, as if all the world needed was a good baker. He meant to do much more than nourish the body with that momentous meal —"I am the bread of life. . . ." He wouldn't permit the people to remain animals and His last word on the subject was spoken to get the strays to see through the bread to God. Men cannot be content with calories and one-a-day vitamins; they are starving for sacrament and no one will be satisfied with any bread beneath belief. "Labour not for the meat which perisheth. . . ."

Christ's supper that day on the hill showed His strength not to distribute bread but to put God in a man's mouth. It was no trick and it is not obsolete. The miracle is merely waiting for us to say, "Lord, give us this bread always."

The feeding of the four thousand is not a dim recollection

of the feeding of the five thousand but a distinct event that Matthew and Mark remember happening at another time. Tradition has felt it represented the Gentiles' turn at Christ's table, as the other story described feeding the Jews. However, Pharisees appear immediately after this passage (8:11-12) and they were not normally found in Gentile territory. This miracle is a parallel of the other, with certain distinguishing features: Jesus doesn't feed the multitude this time until they have been with Him three days; and He starts with seven loaves rather than five, and a few fish instead of two; seven baskets are left over, not twelve. The word for "basket" in both accounts of the story refers to the fisherman's large hamper (σπυρίδας), while the word used for "basket" in the accounts of the feeding of the five thousand refers to a smaller lunch basket men often carried (κοφίνους). After the miracle Jesus and His men got into the boat and rowed to the district of Dalmanutha, a place that cannot be identified. (Perhaps, as Augustine suggests, the problem exists because they, like us, had many names for one place.) This miracle, even more than the first one, emphasizes the thoughtfulness of Jesus: ". . . if I send them away hungry to their homes, they will faint on the way; and some of them have come a long way."

CHAPTER 3

Then he made the disciples embark and go on ahead to the other side, while he sent the people away; after doing that, he went up the hill-side to pray alone. It grew late, and he was there by himself. The boat was already some furlongs from the shore, battling with a head-wind and a rough sea. Between three and six in the morning he came to them, walking over the lake. When the disciples saw him walking on the lake they were so shaken that they cried out in terror: 'It is a ghost!' But at once he spoke to them: 'Take heart! It it I; do not be afraid.' Peter called to him: 'Lord, if it is you, tell me to come to you over the water.' 'Come', said Jesus. Peter stepped down from the boat, and walked over the water towards Jesus. But when he saw the strength of the gale he was seized with fear; and beginning to sink, he cried, 'Save me, Lord.' Jesus at once reached out and caught hold of him, and said, 'Why did you hesitate? How little faith you have!' They then climbed into the boat; and the wind dropped. And the men in the boat fell at his feet, exclaiming, 'Truly you are the Son of God.'

MATTHEW 14:22-33 (ALSO MARK 6:46-52; JOHN 6:14-21),
NEW ENGLISH BIBLE

Walking Upon the Water

AFTER FEEDING FIVE thousand people from a lad's lunch basket, one wonders what Jesus will do next. One does not need to wait very long. Late that very night He frightens His disciples half to death by walking toward them on the water.

One must be almost as rash as Peter himself to plunge into this fathomless portion of the gospel. The scene is a sea of mystery far beyond the depth of any expositor who dares to take it seriously. One must either dismiss the miracle immediately by saying, as some scholars do, that the text may be translated as walking "by the sea" instead of "on the sea," or suspect that the piece is a revolting development that came out of a wild night some sailors had at sea. This chapter is for those whose conscience will no longer let them get away with either one of these well-worn exits. The time has come to stop torturing this text. Let us approach it this time not as rabid inquisitors determined to silence it, but as those who are fair enough to hear its side.

The rest of Scripture, of course, is a sofa compared to the high ceilings in these miracles. Skeptics would like to save these stories for the naive, but naiveté seldom goes out for such an athletic Christ. These miracles may be reserved only for men of courage, for those who have faith that God is more than a mother's lap. Frankly, who wants an effeminate God who can not and never will do anything except nag and preach? The exciting thing about these wonders, bewildering as they are, is that they feature an aggressive and masculine God.

Why should we erase all the reasons why little boys look up to their fathers in fervent admiration, or all they mean when they begin, "I bet my Dad could . . ."? This miracle shows us God in His prime. It shows us that we have a Father in heaven of whom we can be proud, a Father who can do some things we are still too young to do. We must not allow arrogant exegesis to read wrinkles into God by ruling out all His activities. Critics can act like six-year-old boys treating their fathers with indulgent condescension after catching their first fish. Yet, in the vacuum created by the departure of the miracles, how many men are afraid God can't do much of anything?

Have we forgotten how the Psalmist cried that when they heard the Almighty approaching, the hills scampered out of the way like little lambs, high mountains skipped into the sea, and whole rivers turned back to run in the other direction? We have mistaken a Father's modesty for senility. We have discredited Christ's activities as if they were out of bounds for divinity. One big division of the devil's work is to try to shut Jesus out of a man's world and into a sanctuary. He wants Jesus shown only when He is looking sad or sickly, sitting in a chair, holding youngsters in His lap, never exerting Himself. It is all part of the demonic campaign to retire God so that we can run things. And it is only our own sin that hides the fact these miracles emphasize—that God can run circles around us any time He wants to.

A new miracle begins with the statement which closes the one Jesus had just done: "And after he had dismissed the crowds, he went up into the hills by himself to pray." That is what Jesus did between miracles—He visited their birthplace. Somehow the One who buttons His vest with stars, who wears earth as a ring around His little finger, lovingly gave

His Son a lion's share of His authority; and Jesus emerged from those interviews bowed under a weight of glory and borne along on shining wings of peace. A woman can build up her husband from Milquetoast to man by the sheer force of her devotion. King Arthur stirred his knights to such a pitch of inspiration that dragons wilted before the swift rush of their steeds; giants turned green at the sight of their blades. But imagine the Prince Himself dressed in the blinding armor of protecting angels and ordained by God! Is it any wonder that the devil quivered and nature was water in His hands? Would not every atom of creation plead to do the Champion's bidding?

According to Mark's account, "It grew late and the boat was already well out on the water, while he was alone on the land. Somewhere between three and six in the morning, seeing them labouring at the oars against a head-wind, he came towards them, walking on the lake." That's life with Christ out of the picture—men working their heads off but getting nowhere. ". . . without me ye can do nothing."

There are those who refuse their Saviour; few, I think, feel that they could not use one. Eyes go bad without corrective lenses. The most perfect match only makes a perfect mess without more of a homemaker than a man or wife. Who do we think keeps the home fires burning? It makes eyes sore to see little children growing up with no better sense of direction than trying to get ahead, little tots gradually getting the impression that they can get away with a little something like a whole life without God. But their blood soon stains the hands of those who started them thinking that way. Tiny upturned faces without the Son soon turn downward into a crying shame of lost causes. Life ahead of us is nothing but trouble—a pointless, thankless job, with thousands of tedious, absolutely wasted evenings, and headaches at breakfast that hang over into the night—without the Specialist to regenerate the clay. Without God, the thing we get done today will have to be done over again. Unblessed, nothing goes right; the pinnacle of success becomes poisonous.

It is getting late in our lives, in our world, and one of the best pictures ever taken of mankind hangs here in the gospel —a handful of dead-tired men straining in vain at the oars. What a perfect likeness of us all—every family album could use a copy. "Since without Thee we do no good," let us look up with the disciples, despite the darkness, and see if Anyone is walking toward us on the water.

"When the disciples saw him walking on the lake they were so shaken that they cried out in terror: 'It is a ghost.'" The boat was screaming with berserk sailors. Naturally, men always assume that any little noise at night means trouble. It is never the cat, certainly not God—only Eli had the presence of mind to identify God for sleepy young Samuel. Any strange explosion makes us think that hell has broken loose. When the Kingdom comes, no doubt men will jump to the conclusion that the bomb has dropped and will trample each other in the rush for shelter. No one should be surprised to find that the disciples immediately identified Jesus as the devil and began tearing up the night with blood-curdling shrieks. It would be funny if it were not so painfully popular. But panic is one part guilt and two parts doubt. Our "ghost" is not a menace but our good angel; and the "thing" that's waiting for us just around the corner in the dead of night doesn't have our number on it but our Christian name. If we had faith, we would not be a bundle of nerves but would look up and watch the dreadful apparition vanish, and we would hear, instead of a fiend from hell, the Son from heaven: "But at once he spoke to them: 'Take heart! It is I; do not be afraid.'"

". . . walking on the lake. . . ." It is so easy for us to imagine the worst possible thing that could have happened that it is difficult to believe the best. How could anyone have so much mind over matter? Was the uplifting force of His faith greater than gravity? Did faith make Jesus light as a feather or freeze the water into ice? Our dead weight would go to the bottom of the sea. But if He was the Creator's Son, His performance ought not to be shocking. If His Father pinched up mountains and pinned up stars to suit Himself, why couldn't His Son intuitively, inherently, go to the head of the class to apply the fourth and fifth dimensions we are slowly groping for? Christ did not try to explain it; He did not care how it worked. He simply went straight to God by faith instead of taking our well-marked detours.

"Peter called to him: 'Lord, if it is you, tell me to come to you over the water.'" Peter was certainly not the kind to maintain, "None of my family would ever walk on water!" He was impulsive, reckless, and perhaps his pride made him something of a show-off—if Christ could walk around on the water in the dark, he could, too!

This quality of Peter's was precious. He was willing to believe in something new under the sun, ready to believe that he'd been blind. He was eager to live life to the full, to believe there may have been something better beyond him. And he knew the one thing no one else seemed to know—that Christ knew the secret. We know that floating on the water is all a matter of faith—that's how flying started, too—but the feat that night was not working miracles with water, but with Peter's trust.

"Peter stepped down from the boat, and walked over the water towards Jesus. But when he saw the strength of the gale he was seized with fear, and beginning to sink, he cried, 'Save me, Lord.'" Ancient mariners shouted, "Don't look down!" to young landlubbers scuttling up the lanyards to the crow's nest. Simon stared out at the storm and down at his two little feet and fell in. Bystanders shout, "Watch out!" but so many men do nothing else and finally are frozen by the horrors that have caught their eyes forever. Those horrors finally bore holes in faith. The strategy is not to watch out for oneself—people are going mad, going down, with that obsession. To see straight, one has to keep his eyes on Christ, for He alone is infallible. The pathology flourishing about us today is that men can think and talk of nothing else but danger, crime, communism; those people have properly identified the enemy but they can't see Christ for the crisis. Sooner or later, men who can see only the devil and the deep blue sea are sunk. Peter taught us all a lesson that day. Don't watch your step—watch Christ taking His. Facing Christ, we find everything under control; the waves fall back in place. If we cannot get the storm out of our heads, it will soon be our whole world, and it will get bigger and bigger until we are swallowed up. If we cannot think of anything but self-defense, and the ugly face of the enemy in the Kremlin, and the snapshots on the post-office wall, we will become their victims.

Jesus was ready to reach out for Peter as soon as He could get his attention once again. After both got back into the boat, Mark says they all were astounded but their hearts were hardened. John reports no reaction but Matthew recollects that the crew got down and worshiped Christ. These conflicting reports are confusing but they give the story a journalistic freshness and reveal the three reactions readers still have to this miracle. Some men, upon hearing it now, will react negatively, just as Mark described it. They will smile or complain that the Bible asks a man to believe too much and will welcome the tall tale as an excuse to disbelieve the whole Book. This joke is the last straw they've been seeking to break them away from the rest of faith. Others, according to John, will have nothing to say but will go on tomorrow as if it didn't matter whether or not Jesus ever walked on water. Did John's silence mean the men were bored, ready to go to bed? Or was he hoping that we would guess what Matthew said, that after they saw this miracle they all got down on their knees to Christ?

One is constantly amazed to find how many men have entered Christianity through the door of miracles. Pascal quoted Augustine as saying, "I should not be a Christian but for the miracles." Perhaps some reader's faith has waited to begin until he waded into this particular one again. At least this moving scene seemed to Matthew to touch off a cry from all hands on board that night: "Truly you are the Son of God."

CHAPTER 4

That day, in the evening, he said to them, 'Let us cross over to the other side of the lake.' So they left the crowd and took him with them in the boat where he had been sitting; and there were other boats accompanying him. A heavy squall came on and the waves broke over the boat until it was all but swamped. Now he was in the stern asleep on a cushion; they roused him and said, 'Master, we are sinking! Do you not care?' He stood up, rebuked the wind, and said to the sea, 'Hush! Be still!' The wind dropped and there was a dead calm. He said to them, 'Why are you such cowards? Have you no faith even now?' They were awestruck and said to one another, 'Who can this be whom even the wind and the sea obey?'

MARK 4:35-41 (ALSO MATTHEW 8:18, 23-27; LUKE 8:22-25),
NEW ENGLISH BIBLE

Calming the Storm at Sea

THERE ARE NOT many nature-miracles in the gospels, but why did the evangelists let in any of them? Were those fantastic exploits thrown into the New Testament merely to taunt the modern mind? Or was God busy moving heaven and earth together in unusually bold ways while Christ was down here? Can it be that the nature-miracles are native New Testament vegetation? These chapters invite the reader to enjoy that rare presupposition for a moment. After all, the Christian faith has not been feeling too well lately, and a change of theological scenery might do us all some good.

Jesus' crowds were increasing, along with the criticism. He had been caught working again on the sabbath, with incredible results in making both miracles and enemies. "When his family heard of this, they set out to take charge of him; for people were saying that he was out of his mind." Jesus had to carry on with a strange mixture of encouragement and oppositon. After a day spent in preaching from a boat (the beach was mobbed with men) on the Parable of the Sower, He suggested, "Let us cross over to the other side of the lake."

"A heavy squall came on and the waves broke over the boat until it was all but swamped. Now he was in the stern asleep on a cushion. . . ." Could there be any clearer picture of the human predicament than that of men at sea in a storm with

God asleep? Shortly after adolescence we wake up to the grim fact that we have a death sentence hanging over our heads and the ground under our feet is about as firm as water. Men are drowning on all sides of us in alcoholism too endemic to be noticed as a national disaster. For all we know from medical reports, tobacco may be taking its toll. Then there is the cold war between two hemispheres and the dead war within the church; and all this time, homes are breaking up, minds are going to pieces, lives are pouring down the drain. The mortal storm rages inside and out. No one sees any landmarks, for we are in the dark; we don't know where we are or where we'll be tomorrow. We are too drugged and distracted to declare with the Roman gladiators: "We who are about to die salute you." Our situation is impossible, hopeless—Christ is asleep.

"... they roused him and said, 'Master, we are sinking!'" It doesn't seem as if Mark was trying to put one over on us. Remember the last time you were petrified with fear? Not unless you are unusually honest. We repress memories of our cowardice to make room for those delusions of grandeur. Perhaps miracles aren't permitted today because we are so busy fooling ourselves with inflated pretensions of our own abilities. The disciples disarmed the devil with honesty—they were always good at that—not only in confessing how bad they were, which is common, but how green. God never seems competent in our eyes until we discover how incompetent we are behind the false front of the ego. We'll admit to sin but not to uselessness. We don't mind Jesus' being superior to us morally; what we cannot accept is that He can do our jobs better than we can.

Think of the scene at sea. Those husky fishermen knew the sea like a book and you might expect them to have treated their Chaplain with kindly condescension—"You stick to your Sunday-morning moralizing, Reverend, and let us men handle the boat!" No. Those weatherbeaten veterans had the raw courage to advertise to the world that their hard-won sea legs and experience were kid stuff. They admitted (in Scripture) that they had to look to a Carpenter to come to the rescue.

When will it ever occur to some of the D.D.'s, Ph.D.'s, M.D.'s, major generals, and V.I.P.'s that, from the way things look outside and in, they are doing a bum job with the world? The bulging asylums, the jammed hospitals, the gutters clogged with victims, the millions going to bed hungry or overstuffed, offer conclusive evidence of our incompetence. Sigmund Freud's booming voice has drowned out the voice of God, but where are psychology's radiantly happy converts? Preachers are still puttering about irrelevantly, but is all psychiatric tinkering fixing men for good? The streets are not filled with rousing testimonies of thanks for the perfectly lovely therapy at the asylum.

Today, if we'll admit it, we are in the same boat with those desperate disciples. Our crew is a conglomeration of expert politicians, preachers, and corporation presidents, but the ship is sinking, as any child who reads the papers can see. It is grimly humorous to watch the cold-war latecomers throwing stones at Christ from our glass house. Who is kidding whom? When will we experts admit to the mess we've made, and make the opening in our ranks big enough for a Master to move in. Our boat is a preposterous sieve and all hands are helpless in the air.

Does Christ have to be awakened? His nap is a way of saying He won't interfere with our free will. He won't take over unless He's invited. "Master, we are sinking! Do you not care?" His disciples turned to Him as an afterthought, adding a complaint to their delay. But He awoke instantly, clear-headed and in complete command of Himself. Waking Christ, to us, seems like waking the dead; we are not trained to do that. Our alternate brainstorms are consumed as fast as we can dream them up and soon we'll have no other choice but Him.

How do we know He would speak to our situation? Suppose a family, or a village, or a nation, agreed to ask Him to try His hand? Suppose we decided this Sunday to relinquish the reins and wish His will? How could He do any worse than we have done without Him? Someone ought to speak to our planet before it goes any farther. Would not the One who put earth and man together be the very Person to put them back in line? Another aeon wouldn't do any good, but one word from Someone close to God, Someone like Christ, would give us new confidence in creation's chances.

C. S. Lewis agrees that God's earth is not now completely under His control, for good Mother Nature is mixed up with evil. Earth, to some extent, remains the football between two opposing forces, God and the devil. But God is winning and one day plans to do Adam's old homeplace completely over—to redeem it, not throw it away—domesticating its jungle and cleansing the scarlet sea of guilt that bathes it now. It will be a paradise when He gets through, and when He makes the final *coup d'etat* nature will be as docile and subservient all the time as she is every once in a while for Christ. This miracle is an example of the perfect way nature will behave permanently when God has won back His lost paradise, when nature and man are completely in His hands again without any interference from the grave of Lucifer.

Since God's Kingdom has to begin somewhere, God grant us the courage to issue that essential invitation. We are not asked to believe too much. This story doesn't say the disciples knew He could save them, but that they didn't know what else to do. Do we? All they did was turn to Him and give Him the chance. Since no other saviour is offering Him any competition, we could do worse than address the same old cry to that high and tested Source. Surely chaos has not forgotten

who her Master is. If only faith can remember faintly how
to say,

> Be still, my soul: the waves and winds still know
> His voice who ruled them while he dwelt below.

CHAPTER 5

And on the morrow, when they were come from Bethany, he was hungry: And seeing a fig tree afar off having leaves, he came, if haply he might find any thing thereon: and when he came to it, he found nothing but leaves; for the time of figs was not yet. And Jesus answered and said unto it, No man eat fruit of thee hereafter for ever. And his disciples heard it. And they come to Jerusalem: and Jesus went into the temple, and began to cast out them that sold and bought in the temple, and overthrew the tables of the moneychangers, and the seats of them that sold doves; And would not suffer that any man should carry any vessel through the temple. And he taught, saying unto them, Is it not written, My house shall be called of all nations the house of prayer? but ye have made it a den of thieves. And the scribes and chief priests heard it, and sought how they might destroy him: for they feared him, because all the people was astonished at his doctrine. And when even was come, he went out of the city. And in the morning, as they passed by, they saw the fig tree dried up from the roots. And Peter calling to remembrance saith unto him, Master, behold, the fig tree which thou cursedst is withered away. And Jesus answering saith unto them, Have faith in God. For verily I say unto you, That whosoever shall say unto this mountain, Be thou removed, and be thou cast into the sea; and shall not doubt in his heart, but shall believe that those things which he saith shall come to pass; he shall have whatsoever he saith. Therefore I say unto you, What things soever ye desire, when ye pray, believe that ye receive them, and ye shall have them.

MARK 11:12-24 (ALSO MATTHEW 21:18-22), KING JAMES VERSION

Cursing the Fig Tree

JESUS WORKED a miracle early Monday morning of the last week of His life. Yesterday He had been treated royally along shouting streets thickly carpeted with men's coats and children's palm branches. Today He would curse a tree for telling a lie with its leaves, and would clean up the temple till it shone with bristling clergy determined to see Him die. Thus a barren fig tree began the Monday that belonged to Good Friday.

Killing a tree was the only negative miracle Jesus ever did; all the rest of His works were constructive. Tidy scholars are embarrassed by this miracle. After all, Christ has already broken up the sabbath with wonders and they cannot have Him going around swearing at a tree. So, many commentators have dressed up the Bible a bit by squeezing this piece of violence into a harmless little parable. Luke has one that fits—with a little stretching.

We must admit that the uncanonical material contains mountains of this kind of misinformation. The Boy Jesus, in one spurious legend, destroys His playmates with a petulant curse, and those childish outrages in the Apocrypha make our Master look like a monster. But since we have Matthew and Mark to thank for keeping that illicit literature out of their gospels, we must give due respect to the one curse they report.

Of course, it was as common for the rabbis of those days to curse as to bless. Cursing was taken seriously as standard military equipment against the attacks of the devil. Even Elijah invited bears to come out and eat up juvenile delinquents who made fun of him. But Jesus was involved with only one curse, and to His credit it was made, not against a man, but against a tree.

Extreme liberals may run from this incident, but what could be wrong with taking a quick look before it is dogmatically edited out? Some Scripture may not strike a light in us now, but it may fire another's imagination later on in a way a cautious analyst of Scripture will never do. Trench tipped us off to the danger of making up problems: "Those who magnify [differences] into serious difficulties are the true pharisees of history, straining at gnats and swallowing camels."

"On the following day, after they had left Bethany, he felt hungry, and, noticing in the distance a fig-tree in leaf, he went to see if he could find anything on it." Jesus did not spend Palm Sunday night in the city but went next door to Bethany, probably to Mary and Martha who were just getting accustomed to living with their resurrected Lazarus. So Jesus found this fig tree before sun-up Monday morning while returning from suburban Bethany to Jerusalem.

Christ was not putting on a parabolic act with a fig tree. He was hungry, and while it was "not the season for figs" the fig tree was in leaf, which meant it was asking to be picked (some Palestinian fig trees produce fruit first, then leaves). The tree fooled Jesus, but Jesus was not fooling: "May no one ever again eat fruit from you!" Jesus was not blaming the plant for uselessness but was using it to illustrate God's feeling about falseness in human nature. The tree was pretending to bear and He cursed its trickery.

It is not by accident that the cursing of the fig tree was followed by the cleansing of the temple. Something dreadful had happened to Judaism and Jesus went to the heart of it a little later in the morning: "My house shall be called of all nations the house of prayer? but ye have made it a den of thieves." The key to the fig-tree scene is the sin inside the temple. The tragedy was not merely in the temple's impotence but in her pretense of fertility. She dressed in the uniform of faith, decorating her speech sweetly with sacred language, but it was a fake front for a faith that never saw active service. Israel erected a temple which became the perfect place to avoid God. Thanks were subsidized and sin was artificially erased with blood. But the whole ecclesiastical industry was humbug. Religion was a sham of regulations, a rigid code of liturgy chanted, as it were, over God's dead body. Israel acted as if she had the last word; Pharisees gave the impression that they had arrived. But godliness was dead as a door nail. The traffic in the temple was glaring testimony to the orthodox camouflage. Business had propped up the corpse of religion and was getting away with murder. Jesus caught them red-handed in the temple that day. He was angry, not because religion was so idle, but because people were pretending that everything was working beautifully.

Piety had become a manipulated socialistic bureau of sacrifices absolutely guaranteed to supply salvation. The whole slick business was perpetuated to fleece the poor and exploit the innocent. The temple reeked with a land-office business in birds and sheep. The house of prayer had become an auction barn, knee-deep in the mud of steaming animals and a maze of stalls, up to the rafters with screaming vendors getting rich quickly, splitting the profits with priests, cheating under the counter, and coating the palm of the inspector of sacrifices. The gall of calling that slaughterhouse salvation! It drove John the Baptist to the desert. It sent Christ into such a towering rage that He drove them all out. Calling that carnival of extortion the church of the living God made Christ curse. And the miracle of the fig tree is that *it* took His wrath instead of that band of cutthroats who deserved it.

This miracle gives us something more to worry about. Is the church today all she's cracked up to be? Or has she been so busy with bazaars that she has forgotten what happened to the temple? How are we doing? We put up a spire, top it off with a cross, ring a bell, and we're in business. Whose business? Is there nothing more to a church than organizing a choir and hiring a professional? We harp about salvation. Do we have it? Then why do we have such outrageously cheap conversions? One can have a church funeral and his children neatly christened, all for a mumble of incoherent vows, a miscellaneous pledge, and worship in absentia. Or the latest bargain can be kept beautifully outside at the expense of the interior. In the whirl of pronouncements, campaigns for capital funds, and drives for membership, has the church thrown away the keys of the Kingdom? In a moment of despair, T. S. Eliot compared the church unfavorably to a hippopotamus:

> The hippo's feeble steps may err
> In compassing material ends,
> While the true church need never stir
> To gather in its dividends.

> He shall be washed as white as snow,
> By all the martyr'd virgins kist,
> While the true church remains below
> Wrapt in the old miasmal mist.

What kind of mothers are we to our members? We claim to make Christians—When did we make the last one? Who was he? Did we praise God for it? Do we really pray for each other, love each other, comfort and encourage each other in the things that pertain to Christ? Or is it a laugh and are those only words out of a dead past? Is the church a house of prayer, filled with godly men of prayer, singing in the excitement of forgiveness given them, thrilled by the way their children are embracing the faith? How many Good Samaritans make their homes here? Are we looking for the lost sons to come back and sending the seventy out to serve? Or has that high life receded, died down, leaving us like a tree with leaves falling by the bucketful, but no fruit?

We would remind those outside who complain of hypocrites in here that we can always use one more. Nonetheless, we must dread hypocrisy lest Christians become wolves in sheep's clothing. Those who never darken the door of the church are perhaps not as bad off as those who do nothing else. There is a danger in joining the church if we are publishing to the world an association that we do not intend to cultivate, and we can kill the cause with misrepresentation just as men did in Jesus' day. The "whiskey priest" is no worse than the bewhiskered deadwood who whittles down the hickory testimony to a toothpick.

When we identify with Christianity, we take on a terrible risk of being two-faced. It is bad enough to be anti-Christ, without adding the pretense of being the contrary. The fig tree was cursed not for its failure but for its false show of luxuriant green without the nourishing fruit to back it up. Hypocrisy in God's house was the only thing that ever made Christ swear. It ought to be enough to make us wear our Christian affirmation with more care.

That Monday night, going back home to Bethany, it was too dark to check the threatened tree. But the next morning, returning to Jerusalem, "they saw that the fig-tree had withered from the roots up; and Peter, recalling what had happened, said to him, 'Rabbi, look, the fig-tree which you cursed has withered.'" It was like Jesus to dismiss the compliment with an expression of confidence in His disciples and to end the negative miracle on a positive note. What He had done was nothing to the everything they would do: "Have faith in

God. I tell you this: if anyone says to this mountain, 'Be lifted from your place and hurled into the sea', and has no inward doubts, . . . it will be done for him. I tell you, then, whatever you ask for in prayer, believe that you have received it and it will be yours." After such a difficult miracle, Jesus didn't give the disciples a little relief. No, that incident was a jumping-off place for a flabbergasting assignment. Moving swiftly from trees to mountains, He made men dizzy with the fantastic power at faith's fingertips. All they had to do was to have no doubt about it. They could go ahead and make definite plans according to their prayers, as if their requests had already become history.

God would have to be quite a God and one would have to be quite an intimate friend of His to trust Him so far. Christ did and, what's more, He had the astounding nerve to believe we could do better. The password to paradise is prayerful faith. It is the way by which we can hold all nature spellbound, as it will be on the day He sets foot here again. What is He waiting for but our faith, and what is He worried about but our insincerity?

CHAPTER 6

When they reached Capharnahum, the collectors of the temple-tax came and asked Peter, "Does your teacher not pay the temple-tax?" He said, "Yes." But when he went indoors, Jesus spoke first; "Tell me, Simon," he said, "from whom do earthly kings collect customs or taxes? Is it from their own people or from aliens?" "From aliens," he said. Then Jesus said to him, "So their own people are exempt. However, not to give any offence to them, go to the sea, throw a hook in, and take the first fish you bring up. Open its mouth and you will find a five-shilling piece; take that and give it to them for me and for yourself.

MATTHEW 17:24-27, MOFFATT

Finding a Coin in a Fish's Mouth

THIS MIRACLE IS much different and much more difficult than all the other miracles Jesus did to nature. It is a tax matter and Tax-Man Matthew is the only one to bring it up.

"On their arrival at Capernaum the collectors of the temple-tax came up to Peter and asked, 'Does your master not pay temple-tax?' 'He does', said Peter. This question reminds us that the pre-Christian church was supported by dues instead of charity. Each male Israelite who had reached twenty years of age was charged a half shekel annually to keep up the temple. Tolls were levied on goods; tribute money was levied on individuals. Very few Jews objected to giving thirty-five cents to God but they generally resented paying the rent to the Roman force of occupation.

Peter's answer speaks for Jesus' patriotism, not to the political state, but to the theocracy of Judaism. The temple tax was not a federal but a religious tax. Despite comments to the contrary, the incident does indicate Jesus' response to public authority. As revolutionary as He was, He was no anarchist. He obeyed God, not Caesar, but as far as we know, He never found it necessary to violate or subvert the state under which He lived. Pilate found no fault with Him and even the high priest had to break and bend ecclesiastical law in a horseplay of justice to get Him crucified. The mob went mad for His blood partly because He wouldn't lead a militant Messianic rebellion. His followers were persecuted not for poor citizenship but because Caesar started to act like a god.

This gospel story substantiates Jesus as a Man who paid His taxes. The scene, however, focuses on His religious responsibilities. The collector may have been a Roman officer, but there was no threat implied in the situation. The question could have come from curiosity as well as from suspicion and it more likely meant: "How are you related to Judaism? Are you a special case or do you come under the tax requirement, too?" Peter, impetuous as usual, promptly affirmed it without bothering about some serious ramifications that called for a more cautious distinction. Of course, his Master gives to God the things that are God's! Peter jumped to the right conclusion in one respect; Jesus did not come "to destroy but to fulfil" the law. ". . . as his custom was, he went to the synagogue on the sabbath day . . . ," and did not depart from His own interpretation of the faith.

Promising to pay the tax put Jesus in a bad light; it made Him look exactly like any other Jew, and Peter forgot for a minute that Jesus was Christ. His Master was not a religious subject but the ruling Prince. Jesus did not mind making a payment but to do so would deny His identity. The Son of God was not to make an offering; the offering was to be made to Him.

Jesus calmly extricated Himself from the spot on which Peter had placed Him. Once again He knew how to ask the right questions to restore perspective: " 'What do you think about this, Simon? From whom do earthly monarchs collect tax or toll? From their own citizens, or from aliens?' 'From aliens', said Peter. 'Why then,' said Jesus, 'the citizens are exempt!'" Patiently Jesus put His disciples back into that special category, making a distinction between their position and that commonly held by their contemporaries. Christian sons do not owe anything. Paul elaborates on the religious freedom from Old Testament law which Christians enjoy by God's grace. Christ's disciples are not duty-bound but bear their service in benevolence, spontaneously, as the fruit of God's special goodness to men. This story establishes the separation of church and state, as well as testifies to the absurdity of taxing the King and the King's men.

Jesus managed a solution worthy of the Son of Solomon; He satisfied the tax collector and saved Peter or Himself embarrassment: "But as we do not want to cause difficulty for these people, go and cast a line in the lake; take the first fish that comes to the hook, open its mouth, and you will find a silver coin; take that and pay it in; it will meet the tax for us both." Before we come to the miracle, consider the marvel of how beautifully Jesus thought of everyone involved. Peter was included in the payment and the officials were treated as human beings who deserved respect. Yet the debt was paid by a King.

Jesus did these things whenever He wanted to do them. The deeper mystery is how economical He was with miracles and how much they looked like the handiwork of God. This grace-saving feature impressed Bishop Trench:

All attempts to exhaust this miracle of its miraculous element, to make the evangelist tell, and intend to tell, an ordinary transaction, as that of the rationalist Paulus, who will have it that the Lord bade Peter go and catch as many fish as would sell for the required sum, and maintains that this actually lies in the words,—are hopelessly absurd. In an opposite extreme, they multiply miracles without a warrant who assume that the stater was created for the occasion; nay more, they step altogether out of the proper sphere of miracle; in which, as distinguished from the act of pure creation, there is always a nature-basis to which the Divine Power that works the wonder more or less closely links itself. That Divine Power which dwelt in Christ, restored, as in the case of the sick, the halt, the blind; it multiplied, as the bread in the wilderness; it changed into a nobler substance, as the water at Cana; it quickened and revived, as Lazarus and the daughter of Jairus; it brought together, as here, by wonderful coincidences, the already existing; but, as far as our records reach, it formed no new limbs; it made no bread, no wine, out of nothing; it created no new men: never passed over on any occasion into the region of absolute creation.

CHAPTER 7

And it came to pass, that, as the people pressed upon him to hear the word of God, he stood by the lake of Gennesaret, And saw two ships standing by the lake: but the fishermen were gone out of them, and were washing their nets. And he entered into one of the ships, which was Simon's, and prayed him that he would thrust out a little from the land. And he sat down, and taught the people out of the ship. Now when he had left speaking, he said unto Simon, Launch out into the deep, and let down your nets for a draught. And Simon answering said unto him, Master, we have toiled all the night, and have taken nothing: nevertheless at thy word I will let down the net. And when they had this done, they inclosed a great multitude of fishes: and their net brake. And they beckoned unto their partners, which were in the other ship, that they should come and help them. And they came, and filled both the ships, so that they began to sink. When Simon Peter saw it, he fell down at Jesus' knees, saying, Depart from me; for I am a sinful man, O Lord. For he was astonished, and all that were with him, at the draught of the fishes which they had taken: And so was also James, and John, the sons of Zebedee, which were partners with Simon. And Jesus said unto Simon, Fear not; from henceforth thou shalt catch men. And when they had brought their ships to land, they forsook all, and followed him.

LUKE 5:1-11, KING JAMES VERSION

After these things Jesus shewed himself again to the disciples at the sea of Tiberias; and on this wise shewed he himself. There were together Simon Peter, and Thomas called Didymus, and Nathanael of Cana in Galilee, and the sons of Zebedee, and two other of his disciples. Simon Peter saith unto them, I go a fishing. They say unto him, We also go with thee. They went forth, and entered into a ship immediately; and that night they caught nothing. But when the morning was now come, Jesus stood on the shore: but the disciples knew not that it was Jesus. Then Jesus saith unto them, Children, have ye any meat? They answered him, No. And he said unto them, Cast the net on the right side of the ship, and ye shall find. They cast therefore, and now they were not able to draw it for the multitude of fishes. Therefore that disciple whom Jesus loved saith unto Peter, It is the Lord. Now when Simon Peter heard that it was the Lord, he girt his fisher's coat unto him, (for he was naked,) and did cast himself into the sea. And the other disciples came in a little ship; (for they were not far from land, but as it were two hundred cubits,) dragging the net with fishes. As soon then as they were come to land, they saw a fire of coals there, and fish laid thereon, and bread. Jesus saith unto them, Bring of the fish which ye have now caught. Simon Peter went up, and drew the net to land full of great fishes, an hundred and fifty and three: and for all there were so many, yet was not the net broken. Jesus saith unto them, Come and dine. And none of the disciples durst ask him, Who art thou? knowing that it was the Lord. Jesus then cometh, and taketh bread, and giveth them, and fish likewise. This is now the third time that Jesus shewed himself to his disciples, after that he was risen from the dead.

JOHN 21:1-14, KING JAMES VERSION

Catching the Fish

EVERYONE HAS A fish story to tell. The gospel has two: one to call Christ's disciples, and one for their commencement exercises. One catch is the prologue and the other the epilogue to their schooling. Both stories begin with the fish that didn't get away and end with the catch of fishermen who didn't get away. The disciples do their tall tale with a drastically different twist from most sportsmen. They emphasize the time they toiled all night and caught nothing, and join in the applause of a perfect Apprentice who almost broke their nets with fish. These experts do not boast *their* sportsmanship but reveal their fiasco by paying a Layman tribute. That is something of a record for fishermen.

Because of the crowded conditions ashore Jesus went aboard Peter's boat to preach; after He had finished using it as a pulpit He gave the captain the order that has ever since challenged as many soldiers as deep-sea sailors: "Launch out into the deep, and let down your nets. . . ." Peter's boat would make quite an addition to the Smithsonian Institute, crowded as it is with such a precious cargo of memories and having seen so much active service as Christ's chancel. It was His ferry, His bed, His escape, and I think it is not irreverent to say it was His favorite sport.

What would you say if, immediately after his sermon, your minister suggested: "Let's go fishing"? Christ's ministry was spiced with a variety of refreshing extracurricular activities conspicuously absent from the wallflower picture of the preacher that sin likes to perpetuate. Men assume that after the worship service anyone who is subjected to the misery of the minister's company must make post mortem comments on his little masterpiece of woe that morning. Not Jesus—after the benediction, He was ready to sail out into the bay. The typical clergyman with his long face and black looks may not make so healthy an impression. That bookworm air, his flair for fluster, his heavy freight of language quick to give offense or bring on sleep, and those unsportsmanlike robes, answer "No"—as though he would not like nor have time to go fishing.

The Master was never dressed up; He preached and fished in the same clothes, and looked much more at home in a boat than behind a desk. While godliness fit Him like a glove, so did God's out-of-doors. He kept close, not only to God and man, but to nature. A minister could use a hive of bees under glass in his study, or keep a few sheep, if he wants to see straight and stay sound. Jesus kept the door open to the woods, to the water. He was heavenly because He was so down to earth and because He did not have a one-track mind. He was flexible, teachable, ready to relinquish His carpenter's shop to appreciate Peter's and John's sea.

"Master, we were hard at work all night and caught nothing at all . . ."; that is to say, "Master, we, who are old hands at this, sifted the sea all night when fish are supposed to bite, and nothing doing." God's good ideas often seem so wild to wild men. Could God's thoughts be higher and more practical than our precious horse-sense? Isn't that the story of our lives, the glaring evidence that we need someone better qualified to assume command? A handful of fishermen learned the folly of man uncaptained, all in a night's work. Without Christ, are we all killing time, no matter how fast the fan mail is pouring in? In the eyes of the Master Fisherman, what have we come up with in life that's so wonderful? What we were told were trophies are engraved tin cans, and what our big eyes thought were fish may be too small to keep and must be thrown back in. Sooner or later each man finds to his distress or happiness that "Except the Lord build the house, they labour in vain that build it. . . ."

Under his breath Simon may have murmured something about landlubbers but he gave Christ the chance to show His true colors. God doesn't require faith always—all He needed then was a little obedience. Ananias couldn't see visiting Saul but that didn't stop him, nor God. Perhaps some wonder is waiting now, under our very noses, for a little action instead of optimism. All a miracle needed was Peter's cooperation: ". . . but if you say so, I will let down the nets."

"They did so and made a big haul of fish; and their nets began to split. . . . [and they] loaded both boats to the point of sinking." There is a miracle of modesty; nothing supernatural could be more natural. Fish do not fall down from the clouds nor fly in over the sides of the boat. Jesus willed them where He wanted them. The miracle was not in His ingenuity but in His authority. Nature gave in to the power of prayer and Jesus lured the fish without the trick of bait. If they came when He called, that was not out of line with the Creator's intention: "Thou madest him [man] to have dominion. . . . thou hast put all things under his feet: . . . The fowl of the air, and the fish of the sea, and whatsoever passeth through the paths of the seas."

"When Simon Peter saw it, he fell down at Jesus' knees, saying, Depart from me; for I am a sinful man, O Lord." Peter was not terrified because the ship was sinking, but because he identified the miracle. A nearsighted man would have missed the point, but Simon was sharp enough to sense a far superior hand in the catch than his or Lady Luck's. It was too beautiful, too perfect to take sitting down; so they quickly got down on their knees.

Strangers cannot understand how God can scare anybody. They do not know God nor human nature. Sin will run from holiness every time, and infinity frightens the finite. If your favorite star takes your breath away, what about the Emperor of the universe? We would approach the throne shaking, not for fear of what He might do, but because of things we've done, the way we're dressed inside, which grows shocking by comparison. The miracle made Peter feel guilty. He was acutely aware of the depressing gulf between all that's right with God and wrong with us. God means to make men like Him, but when He begins we are light years apart and holiness simply prostrates profanity: ". . . let not God speak with us, lest we die."

"At moments like these," as Trench tells it, "all that is merely conventional is swept away, and the deep heart utters itself, and the deepest things that are there come forth to light." C. S. Lewis says that the day of judgment will arrive when "God switches on all the lights." Under God's ultraviolet rays our hidden faults and best-kept secrets will show up and we will almost die from the exposure. There will be a blinding moment of consciousness while our lives are getting adjusted to the light—and that was the piercing, shaming Son who was just dawning on Peter.

" 'Do not be afraid,' said Jesus to Simon; 'from now on you will be catching men.' " Thank God, Jesus didn't depart as Simon suggested, for Simon's total depravity was the occasion for his ministry, not a drawback to make him ineligible. It is because God is good and we are not that we cannot afford to let Him go. To say, "I'm not good enough for God," is to sigh, "I'm too sick to go to the hospital." Peter's humiliating admission paved the way for his inauguration into discipleship. It ordained all hands on that rude deck to do the job on the rest of us.

Why did Jesus go down to the dock to do His recruiting when the palaces were packed with kings and illustrious campuses were piled high with Plato's and Seneca's descendants? Perhaps it is easier to educate the uneducated; God can do more with men who know how much is wrong with them and how much has to be done. God began at the bottom layer of humanity and not with some pompous Aristotle or Alexander. God meant, as Augustine explained, "to draw emperors to himself by fishermen, and not fishermen by emperors, lest his church should even seem to stand in the wisdom and power of men rather than of God." Anyone can tell at a glance, by the inferior caliber of the "help," that any good coming out of the church has to be God.

What a relief to find God speaking our language—we do not have to learn His! Christ did not speak in Greek but in the vernacular Aramaic. He did not try to be an incomprehensible theologian. He sounded like a fisherman speaking to fishermen. God's Son came down to where His men were and met them at their level. He approached different men differently and outlined His plans in their terms.

It was not the first time Jesus had fished for these men; it was the day He landed them. They had been running with the hook long enough. Every now and then some Paul is pulled up in a fury of immediacy—John Donne nicknamed them "fusile apostles"—but Jesus gave those men all the line they wanted and reeled them in when they were ready. The catch of fish was merely the bait He used to finish off the long haul of fishermen.

The fish became the favorite symbol of the first church. Jesus could have insisted upon using only the tools of His own trade; instead He gave His fishermen that honor. It is much better to fish for men than to hunt for them. The hunter shoots to kill; the fisherman takes his game alive. And preaching is more like using a net than a pole. Christianity is not after one, but everyone. It is angling for a family, a congregation, a community—not merely a stray. Christianity is coaxing creatures up out of the cold-blooded deep into another element.

God has gone fishing for several thousand years to see if He could catch some sons. He made a net from fishermen and mended it with martyrs. We call it a church—and it's been cut and torn—but it was created to dredge the world and scoop up men, to get them to break the surface of their selfishness and come up into a sky-blue heaven. The fish symbolizes our belief that men do not belong below, but above with Him. If we get near His ship, our time may come, for God is a good Fisherman.

"As soon as they had brought the boats to land, they left everything and followed him." The prospect who promises he'll be back is a poor risk, and the determined evangelist gets commitments before the revival breaks up. "I'll think about it" isn't very substantial, for devotion is related to eagerness. The only disciples who are any good are those who cannot wait to get to shore to start. Peter didn't sell his boat; he didn't throw the nets overboard, for he went fishing again after the resurrection. "Leaving everything" refers to the soul's revolution. The Master met those men doing work that was not wrong, but outranked, and they signed on under a new Superior. Becoming a Christian does not necessarily require a moving van and a new letterhead. The change takes place inside the man; the same old thing looks different because of the new lighting effect and the fresh view one gets from the other side of allegiance. God will transform us, not the geography, bringing the old routines to life and supercharging the old skills.

The "everything" the disciples left was their old selves; they were freed from that "almighty me," ready for an adventure under a Pilot who knew His celestial navigation. Augustine appreciated how big the sacrifice was: "These Apostles might have left little when they left their possessions; but they left much, and had a right to feel they had left much, when they left their desires."

John's fish story cannot be superimposed over Luke's. Both stories stand beautifully by themselves and look best side by side, despite their similarities. John surely saw the first fish story firmly fixed in Luke when he decided to add his for a finishing touch. His is too good a story, too perfect a setting, not to be told. The disciples dated their ordination from the first fishing trip; the second one sealed their ministry and inspired it for the duration.

In John's story it was Peter who launched the boat: "I'm going fishing." It was not forbidden, and he had not forgotten how. In a downswell of emotion following the resurrection, he turned naturally to the sea to do something with his hands. The rabbis had their manual trades for psychological as well as economic reasons. Paul had his tents to turn to, Peter his lifeboat.

"But that night they caught nothing. Morning came, and there stood Jesus on the beach," unrecognized. "'Friends, have you caught anything?' They answered 'No.'" Was the figure ashore a customer? The cry came again like a tonic to despair: "Shoot the net to starboard, and you will make a catch." The voice had the ring not only of authority but of contagious confidence. (The right side in Scripture symbolizes the right side morally; the sheep are on His right side, the place of honor.) Did they believe? No, I think they obeyed because they had nothing better to do. Why not take His suggestion? "They did so, and found they could not haul the net aboard, there were so many fish in it. Then the disciple whom Jesus loved said to Peter, 'It is the Lord.' When Simon Peter heard that, he wrapped his coat about him (for he had stripped) and plunged into the sea." John was the first to perceive, Peter the first to act.

"When they came ashore, they saw a charcoal fire there,

with fish laid on it, and some bread. Jesus said, 'Bring some of your catch.' Simon Peter went aboard and dragged the net to land, full of big fish, a hundred and fifty-three of them. . . . Jesus said, 'Come and have breakfast.' None of the disciples dared to ask 'Who are you?' They knew. . . . Jesus now came up, took the bread, and gave it to them, and the fish in the same way." Jesus took His last turn as Host—or His first, depending upon how you look at it. Cooking out was something, even for a sacrament—and it was just like fishermen to give us the exact count of their historic catch.

This is the last miracle, the last memory of Jesus that John leaves us. Who could have finished the four gospels with more finesse? The first miracle was made at a wedding. The last one, instead of at sunset, was held at dawn down on the beach amid high spirits breakfasting in the fresh morning air. Jesus wanted them to enjoy one last catch together before they adjourned, to brief them on resurrection living and assist them by this illustration to make a mammoth transition. His new habitat was not so alien. He still loved their old boat, still loved to fish as in the flesh, and was just as excited over the catch as they were. He didn't disapprove of their fishing now that He was exalted, and He gave them a final miracle to remember before He put out to sea, leaving them in command of the ship.

"After breakfast, Jesus said to Simon Peter, 'Simon son of John, do you love me more than all else?' 'Yes, Lord,' he answered, 'you know that I love you.' 'Then feed my lambs', he said." After the first catch Peter was asked to fish for men; after the last one he was to shepherd them. The first time he was called to duty, finally to devotion. Christ asked Peter to do His chores for Him, and left with this warning: ". . . when you were young you . . . walked where you chose; but when you are old you will stretch out your arms, and a stranger will bind you fast, and carry you where you have no wish to go."

In the beginning the disciples had learned to work for Christ; eventually they were to suffer for Him before they would breakfast new again in the Kingdom of God. Peter was not to worry because John was not included in the warning. A white-haired John, writing his gospel long after all the others were gone, took his last drop of ink to put Peter completely back in place where he was before his earlier fall from grace that fateful Thursday night. These last lines help to keep alive the legend of a Peter who paid nobly for the lambs in pain of a death that was upside down. They remind us as we read today that the cross must come before the crown.

·II·

The
Healing
of the Body

CHAPTER 8

On another occasion when he went to synagogue, there was a man in the congregation who had a withered arm; and they were watching to see whether Jesus would cure him on the Sabbath, so that they could bring a charge against him. He said to the man with the withered arm, 'Come and stand out here.' Then he turned to them: 'Is it permitted to do good or to do evil on the Sabbath, to save life or to kill?' They had nothing to say; and, looking round at them with anger and sorrow at their obstinate stupidity, he said to the man, 'Stretch out your arm.' He stretched it out and his arm was restored. But the Pharisees, on leaving the synagogue, began plotting against him with the partisans of Herod to see how they could make away with him.

MARK 3:1-6 (ALSO MATTHEW 12:1-14; LUKE 6:1-7),
NEW ENGLISH BIBLE

Now when he entered the house of a ruler who belonged to the Pharisees to take a meal, they watched him closely. In front of him there was a man who had dropsy; so Jesus asked the jurists and Pharisees, "Is it right to heal on the sabbath or not?" They held their peace. Then Jesus took hold of the man and cured him and sent him off. "Which of you," he said to them, "when an ass or an ox has fallen into a well, will not pull him out at once upon the sabbath day?" This they could not dispute.

LUKE 14:1-6, MOFFATT

*After this there was a festival of the Jews, and Jesus went up
to Jerusalem. Now there is in Jerusalem near the Sheepgate a
pool called in Hebrew Bethzatha, which has five colonnades.
In these there used to lie a great number of people who were
sick, blind, lame, or paralyzed. There was one man there who
had been sick for thirty-eight years. Jesus saw him lying there,
and finding that he had been in this condition for a long time,
said to him, "Do you want to get well?" The sick man answered,
"I have nobody, sir, to put me into the pool when the water stirs,
but while I am getting down someone else steps in ahead of me."
Jesus said to him, "Get up, pick up your mat, and walk!" And
the man was immediately cured, and he picked up his mat and
walked. Now it was the Sabbath. So the Jews said to the man who
had been cured, "It is the Sabbath, and it is against the Law for
you to carry your mat." But he answered, "The man who cured
me said to me, 'Pick up your mat and walk.' " They asked him,
"Who was it that said to you, 'Pick it up and walk'?" But the
man who had been cured did not know who it was, for as there
was a crowd there, Jesus had left the place. Afterward Jesus
found him in the Temple, and said to him, "See! You are well
again. Give up sin, or something worse may happen to you."
The man went and told the Jews that it was Jesus who had
cured him. This was why the Jews used to persecute Jesus,
because he did things like this on the Sabbath. But he answered
them, "My Father is still at work, and I work too."*

JOHN 5:1-17, GOODSPEED

The Man With the Withered Hand

The Man With Edema

The Cripple by the Pool

TODAY, THE DOCTOR'S reputation far outranks that of the minister. Medicine has been made Queen of the Sciences. Our idea of heroism happens in gleaming operating rooms under the skillful hands and behind the sterile masks of our own Ben Caseys. The word of a specialist carries a lot of weight in court as well as in a hospital.

We have forgotten how foreign this is to history; medicine moved to the seat of honor only yesterday. Before Christ, illness was something that "served you right" and every pagan knew that pain was a dirty trick pulled on him by some spiteful god. "The Gods," as Leslie Weatherhead writes, "were interested only in the healthy. This met human need so inadequately that it is not surprising that Esculapius, the God of Healing, amongst all the Pagan Gods, held out longest against Christianity." Pre-Christian healing efforts were faint and far between. Hippocrates (460 B.C.) stuck out like a sore thumb in his time; and even he is known as an encyclopedist and for his oath, not as a successful practitioner. Hippocrates made almost no impression on Plato, and we know next to nothing about him.

"Until [Christ] came, the orthodox Rabbinical teaching—with some variations . . . —was that since disease is God's will, to heal is an act of impiety. Medical science was disapproved of by Jewish leaders." Well-educated Jews diagnosed sickness as sin's symptom. Job's comforters claimed he only got what was coming to him. Lepers were untouchable. "Jesus's healing was a scandal on a weekday, let alone on the Sabbath." We who live in the second half of the twentieth century can scarcely appreciate the shock Christ's flourishing practice gave the unhygienic status quo. "The miracles of healing. . . . herald a new age."

Jesus healed almost half His identified New Testament patients on the sabbath, including the three singled out for emphasis in this chapter. Since Jesus was not afraid to be different on the sabbath, the issue swiftly became a big bone of contention between Him and His "betters," the Pharisees. Men do not agree which (sabbath) miracles came first, if it matters. But it was plain that the Pharisees intended to make His sabbath "malpractice" a test case when His disciples were caught nibbling grain as they went through a field. There was nothing wrong with helping yourself to lunch from a farmer's field in those days—except on the sabbath. In fact, there was nothing wrong with feasting on the sabbath if the food had been prepared previously—but obviously the disciples were picking and threshing those pinches of grain in their cheeks.

Jesus defended His men too well for their own good, or so it seemed on the surface, and it didn't relieve the situation when Jesus beat the Pharisees at their own game. The sabbath was as dear to Him as to them but He outclassed them in competition. Jesus justified His violation by an impressive familiarity with the primary sources. When the Pharisees attacked Him for letting His men shuck corn on the sabbath, He racked their brains by recalling the time David treated himself to the high priest's holy bread. The Pharisees had learned the commandment backwards; He turned it right side up: "The sabbath was made for man, and not man for the sabbath." Though they couldn't go that far, He put something into the record for anyone listening in later on: ". . . the Son of Man is sovereign even over the Sabbath."

We won't feel the full force of these miracles, however, until we appreciate the grave peril in which they placed the Physician. Jesus did not spend His Sunday afternoons performing in a ballpark; He performed a kindness in the face of a defiant lynch mob. Much of the miracle is in the risk He took, and the miracle becomes even more realistic when we see how He did it in the midst of a hair-raising setting. His therapy becomes pretty convincing as we see how it had to be carried on in the teeth of hostility. I take it as proof of the miracles' historicity that the opposition used the accomplished fact of the remarkable recoveries as decisive evidence against Jesus. We discuss Jesus' greatness and His goodness too generally; it is also unfair to discuss Him simply as a Physician. When He rescued men, He was like a soldier directly in the line of fire.

Matthew reports that Jesus "went on to another place, and entered their synagogue. A man was there with a withered arm and they asked Jesus, 'Is it permitted to heal on the Sabbath?' (Their aim was to frame a charge against him.)" The situation seemed arranged, as if the poor victim had been skimmed off the surrounding sea of misery to tempt Christ to help him on a holy day.

The Pharisees covered their intent to kill with a loaded question. Jesus uncovered their plot by putting the previous question: "Is it lawful on the sabbath . . . to save life or to kill?" The ecclesiastical rascals were hoping He would be kind so they could kill Him for breaking their little bag of rules. But none of them could answer His question without siding with Him or the devil, so they kept still. They eventually managed His murder but He had made their "monkey business" look ridiculous. Jesus was irresistibly eloquent: "What man of you, if he has one sheep and it falls into a pit on the sabbath, will not . . . lift it out? Of how much more value is a man than sheep!" Jesus was so right, but they didn't care about God and men; they wanted to keep their own skin of power stretched tightly over their precious code. He was only a Carpenter against an entrenched Goliath, but He was one Man they couldn't scare or stop, dead or alive: ". . . he looked around them with anger, grieved at their hardness of heart. . . ." Then He snapped their little sabbath locket, retrieving the sabbath God meant man to have. It was an expensive operation.

"Stretch out your hand"—that was asking a lot of a paralyzed man who might not have been able to move a muscle in his arm. But Jesus had a right to expect much from His patient, for He was putting a lot into him. Luke reports that the right hand was withered and, "according to Jerome, the Gospel according to the Hebrews described the man as a mason." If that was so, the handicap was severe and Jesus, being a Builder Himself, must have felt a special tug at His heartstrings. Weatherhead catalogs this cure under the power of suggestion, but the word "suggestion" hardly fits a command from such a powerful Man as Christ. Anyone who had withered the authorities with such a brilliant fire of eloquence must have struck the maimed fellow with the staggering impact of a revelation.

We have no way of knowing whether there were psychological factors involved, or whether the man's hand had been crushed under one of Pilate's hurried building projects. But we unmake this miracle if we try to make it ordinary. We have the honor to present its majesty. We do not jump to diagnosis; we simply do not have a good X ray and we do not need one. The point is, the mason had a useless right hand.

Men in general improve in an atmosphere of faith. Christ always had a shattering effect on despair; being with Him was re-creation. He had a way of giving men self-confidence instead of sterilizing them in their inferiority, as superiority can sometimes do. Imagine how much better everyone felt in the integrating presence of Someone who appreciated them. Certainly the effect of His complete attention would be electrifying, and a wounded hand would have every reason to hasten to please Someone so close to the Father as His Son —especially when His request was so conservative. Nothing abnormal was asked, no magic. Christ simply pulled Himself together in an intensity of prayer to mobilize His mysterious faculty until His power, multiplied many times over, unfolded in a fury of kindness for the sake of a suffering man. The only unusual thing about the result was the terrific acceleration of recovery: " 'Stretch out your arm.' He stretched it out, and it was made sound again like the other."

"But they were filled with fury . . . ," "and immediately held counsel with the Herodians . . . how to destroy him." Jesus left His mark on the sabbath day and He would have to pay. The leading Jews, like malignant Machiavellis, collaborated with the Romans to erase the hand and Him.

"One Sabbath he went to have a meal in the house of a leading Pharisee; and they were watching him closely." The plot thickens. Again He was ambushed by plainclothesmen waiting to witness to His incriminating wonders. No doubt the dinner invitation was a frame-up: "There, in front of him, was a man suffering from dropsy"; and the Physician was perfectly aware of what the authorities were going to do if He made a move to help the man.

Only Luke lists this case, and like a doctor he diagnoses it; today we call the affliction edema. Either term means that water was dammed up in the tissues of the man's arms or legs, blowing them up like balloons. The swelling is common to many sicknesses, often beginning at the ankles. Perhaps the man was an aging Pharisee suffering from cardiac failure, or an alcoholic bum with cirrhosis of the liver who had been dragged in off the streets through the open side of the almost-public dining rooms of those days. Jesus did not tell the man to stay off his feet or prescribe a salt-free diet; He had no dehydration pills to give him. There was something more fundamentally amiss than poor circulation and Jesus went behind the scenes of biology to tie the man's umbilical cord invisibly to God. He did not describe the case as edema; it seemed to Him that somehow the man had stumbled into a pit, and He ran to help him as anyone might have done. "Then Jesus took hold of the man and cured him and sent him off." "To this they could find no reply."

"Later on Jesus went up to Jerusalem for one of the Jewish festivals." Only John reports what wonders went on in the city; and after considering several other possibilities, Trench concludes that this particular celebration must have been "the mother of all other feasts, the Passover." The text doesn't say whether it was Jesus' last or next-to-last Passover.

"Now there is in Jerusalem by the sheep gate a pool, in Hebrew called Bethzatha, which has five porticoes." The porches, or colonnades, were covered with invalids who coveted a chance to bathe in the miraculously curative qualities attributed to the pool, particularly at the periodic intervals when the waters churned. The King James Version at this point follows an ancient manuscript which explained a local superstition: "For an angel went down at a certain season into the pool, and troubled the water: whosoever then first after the troubling of the water stepped in was made whole of whatsoever disease he had."

John noticed that the steps were crawling with "a multitude of invalids, blind, lame, paralyzed." "Among them was a man who had been crippled for thirty-eight years." The King

James Version's word for him was "impotent," which doesn't apply in the way we use the term now; the man's affliction was not impotence but paralysis. "When Jesus saw him lying there and was aware that he had been ill a long time, he asked him, 'Do you want to recover?'" It was not a foolish question, for after a while sick men often lose the longing to get well which is so essential to their cure. How many neuroses are perpetuated unconsciously in wishful thinking? Apparently hope was not quite dead in this man but the spirit of the place had not been very solicitous of him nor fair to his seniority: " 'Sir,' he replied, 'I have no one to put me in the pool when the water is disturbed, but while I am moving, someone else is in the pool before me.'" Quite obviously this lump of despair lacked a Saviour.

"Jesus saith unto him, Rise, take up thy bed, and walk. And immediately the man was made whole, and took up his bed, and walked. . . ." The command is a shock treatment to us—as it was to that man. More difficult to arouse than the atrophied muscles must have been the force of habit frozen in thirty-eight years of conditioning. No one had ever tried such treatment on him before—suddenly someone picked him out of a mountain of misery, and for the first time he knew how it felt to be loved. His heart beat faster; something struck him and everything about him went into action. He saw those eyes and thought he heard the word "Rise." Surely the skies had fallen in! Something thrilled that suspended animation on those steps and a barely breathing greasemark came to life. Before he knew what had happened, he found himself getting up and going home, and his Physician was gone.

". . . the same day was the sabbath." The quick-stepping man going down the road didn't mind carrying his bed; it was not a four-poster but a collapsible pallet, and his heart had never been lighter. But some Pharisees happened to see him and it interrupted their lovely train of thought. Their complaint brought him back down to earth: "You are not allowed to carry your bed on the Sabbath." Their comment must have seemed about as apropos to a cured man as a fly on his ear. Pharisees had thrown another wrench into the heart of Jesus' kindness, but the man did not mean to get his Doctor into trouble when he identified Him later in the temple. He wanted to give credit where credit was due. That is how they ran across each other again in church, and how he happened to get the benefit of Jesus' benediction: ". . . sin no more. . . ." We don't know what sin he had done, but sin causes its share of sickness and it does not seem out of place for a Man of God to pardon His patient.

Why didn't Jesus take care of the rest of the human wreckage festering there by the pool? He didn't have time to do everything and one is amazed that He did so much while the Pharisees were hustling Him off to a cross. But this Physician was not supposed to be a general practitioner; He did all He could, but He was sent here mainly to set the stage for our salvation.

CHAPTER 9

While he was in one of the cities, there came a man full of leprosy; and when he saw Jesus, he fell on his face and besought him, "Lord, if you will, you can make me clean." And he stretched out his hand, and touched him, saying, "I will; be clean." And immediately the leprosy left him. And he charged him to tell no one; but "go and show yourself to the priest, and make an offering for your cleansing, as Moses commanded, for a proof to the people." But so much the more the report went abroad concerning him; and great multitudes gathered to hear and to be healed of their infirmities. But he withdrew to the wilderness and prayed.

LUKE 5:12-16 (ALSO MATTHEW 8:1-4; MARK 1:40-45),
REVISED STANDARD VERSION

In the course of his journey to Jerusalem he was travelling through the borderlands of Samaria and Galilee. As he was entering a village he was met by ten men with leprosy. They stood some way off and called out to him, 'Jesus, Master, take pity on us.' When he saw them he said, 'Go and show yourselves to the priests'; and while they were on their way, they were made clean. One of them, finding himself cured, turned back praising God aloud. He threw himself down at Jesus's feet and thanked him. And he was a Samaritan. At this Jesus said: 'Were not all ten cleansed? The other nine, where are they? Could none be found to come back and give praise to God except this foreigner?' And he said to the man, 'Stand up and go on your way; your faith has cured you.'

LUKE 17:11-19, NEW ENGLISH BIBLE

Cleansing of a Leper

Ten Lepers

LEPROSY IS about the worst thing life can think up to do to man. No other disease can touch its hideous talent for mixing agony with horror. It strikes a small spot on the skin silently, like a viper, and no one notices it until the dreaded numbness sets in and the deathly snow-white color gives it away. Then the victim is subjected to a savage siege of terror as the killer advances slowly, relentlessly, spreading like a venomous stain, finger by finger, often erasing the face first, leaving behind a messy trail of ugly scabs and sores like open sewers. The hands are frozen into claws long before they drop off. The feet boil up into bandaged stumps before they are left behind. The leper's voice breaks into a cracked record of its former self and his features draw tight into the infamous leonine look until they too leave. The flesh rots off, bones give up, inch by creeping inch. Where it stops, nobody knows. In odor and appearance, leprosy has no competitor.

No wonder this illness was selected by tradition as the dirty sign of God's damnation. And so, far worse than the physical torment was the stiff competition leprosy gave hell. Lepers loathed themselves and were abhorrent to society, not because their disease was slightly contagious and nice people could not bear the sight, but because the affliction branded them like the mark of Cain. Lepers had to leave home for good and accept exile forever in desolate colonies of perpetual isolation, not because they were terribly sick, but because they had fallen victim to the devil's dirtiest practical joke. Leprosy was fatal morally. That is why lepers were cruelly stranded without the dignity of prison bars and the security of a warden's care.

Lepers had to stay so many paces away from everyone and shout the warning wherever they went: "Unclean, unclean!" Healing a leper was considered by the rabbis in the same breath with raising the dead, although starvation or some secondary infection such as tuberculosis probably beat many cases of leprosy to the final punch. The leper was ineligible for forgiveness, forbidden to kindness. He had enthusiasm for death only. The inferno would have been a relief for those untouchables.

According to Matthew, "When he [Jesus] came down from the mountain, great crowds followed him; and behold, a leper came to him and knelt before him. . . ." It was immediately after the Sermon on the Mount; perhaps the leper had been listening from a distance and got the impression that this Doctor was a little different. When he saw a break in the crowds, he decided to make a run for it. He got to Jesus just ahead of a centurion whose son was dying.

The leper's case made Mark's first chapter. Luke said it happened in a certain city and he saw, with his more practiced eye for clinical details, that the leper was not suffering from a few spots but was "covered with leprosy." The patient was in no position to make a formal request and would never have been allowed to keep an appointment. It isn't easy for a leper to get up once he gets down, but Luke, looking carefully, could tell that the man was determined to teach courtesy a lesson, whatever it cost: ". . . when he saw Jesus, he fell on his face and besought him. . . ."

"Lord," he said, "if you will, you can make me clean." We cannot imagine Jesus saying, "I will not." There was nothing Jesus would rather do than sweep the pitiful into His arms and take them away to comfort. He did not agree that eyesores should be zoned, and always made a point of being at home to helplessness. This distinguishes Him from us more than His success in surgery. The blurted request from a man beaten to a pulp, a man who had to struggle to keep back the tears, struck Jesus where He lived. It was a big opportunity; there was plenty of trust. All the man needed was a touch of God, and Jesus' heart and hand went out before the Pharisees could summon the police to prevent the crime of contaminating contact.

An untouchable had been touched. Jesus had gotten used to living with outcasts and gotten into the habit of healing the incurable and loving the unlovable. Jesus' reply came after the risk He took: "I will: be thou clean." The man hadn't asked to be healed but to be decontaminated. Somehow Jesus was able to share with the man the extra health and immunity He had against the plague. The exchange was swift and thorough. The remedy was all wrapped up with faith and forgiveness, the prayer of a desperate man, and the love of an Almighty God. "And immediately the leprosy left him, and he was made clean."

Then Jesus "dismissed him with this stern warning: 'Be sure you say nothing to anybody.'" Why the secrecy? Apparently Jesus didn't need any publicity to prove His healing power, but there was more than modesty in the command. One practical matter was that if the episode ever got around, Jesus would have been drowned in a deluge of lepers. Perhaps, since He came to save the whole world and not to operate a leprosarium, He thought He'd better swear the man to secrecy. Loving lepers was prohibited, and His good deed would grind the teeth of religious taxidermists. And so, to save them strain and to play it their way as well as He could,

He said, "Go and show yourself to the priest, and make the offering laid down by Moses for your cleansing; that will certify the cure." Jesus was working through traditional channels. Healing the man was one matter; the main thing was to get him officially cleared so that he could be accepted back into society. His re-entry required that he pass a priest's inspection and make "a gift of two birds, one of which was slain and the other released, as part of the disinfection ceremony."

The man was in no shape to keep quiet about the cure and babbled like a newborn babe. He "made the whole story public; he spread it far and wide, until Jesus could no longer show himself in any town, but stayed outside in the open country. Even so, people kept coming to him from all quarters." The patient didn't pay the price that Jesus asked and his disobedience penalized the Physician by robbing Him of the little peace and quiet He had left. But He did not complain; characteristically, "he withdrew to the wilderness and prayed."

Our only other glimpse of leprosy in the gospels comes in Luke, when Jesus was going to Jerusalem for the last time: ". . . he was travelling through the borderlands of Samaria and Galilee," and the geography enhances the drama of this miracle. Jews had treated Samaritans like lepers for ages. Their severe racial prejudice was off to a good start when Israelites refused to permit Samaritans to take part in the construction of the second temple because of their supposed mongrel blood. That forced the Samaritans to interpret Mt. Gerizim as "the chosen place" for worship, instead of Mt. Zion. Fury over the division of opinion lashed out especially at Passover time when pilgrims were particularly aware of the anathema. "Josephus (Ant. XX.6-1) related the massacre by the Samaritans of a great number of Galilean Pilgrims, which happened a little later than this" trip Jesus was making.

"And as he entered a village, he was met by ten lepers, who stood at a distance and lifted up their voices and said, 'Jesus, Master, have mercy on us.'" The chorus croaked pitifully, keeping their distance respectfully, expectantly. They must have been a strange and mangy fraternity, but once they had been men. They had heard something about Christ, or saw something in Him that made them decide not to ask for a coin; it seemed about time to ask for everything. The desire to get well might be excusable in His eyes. They guessed right. He could not stand to have them stay that way any longer, and so He quickly made a promise to them in His Father's place: "'Go and show yourselves to the priests.' And as they went they were cleansed."

"Then one of them, when he saw that he was healed, turned back, praising God with a loud voice. . . ." Only one —thankfulness is a very rare phenomenon. Etiquette requires that manners be heavily sprinkled with "thanks," but true thanksgiving is not a courtesy. It is a spirit. It is the miracle that happens when a man decides to appreciate the world instead of biting at it or being greedily oblivious to it. Thanks is the height of enjoyment that comes when a man agrees that God is being too good to him. The rest of the men went on their way without leprosy but without the ability to appreciate the cure and Him. One of them got well enough to *enjoy* good health and the first thing he did was turn back before he burst with admiration. As soon as his voice came, it began to bless—Luke's description lets us see how precious it became to him to sing his Saviour's praises. He did not step up to Jesus with his hand out or a neatly printed note; "He threw himself down at Jesus' feet and thanked him."

The rest "slipped away," as Calvin suggests, "to banish the memory of the disease." That was perfectly natural—Who wants to see the doctor again and be reminded of horrible associations? "Let's get out of here!" Ten requests for mercy to one *Te Deum* is about par for prayer. The humiliating thing about the miracle was that the leper who came back was the man no one expected, for it was the same as saying "convict" or "Communist" when Luke said, "And he was a Samaritan."

Good health is not the absence of symptoms but the beating of a thankful heart. Satisfied, Jesus said, "Stand up and go on your way; your faith has cured you." Jesus saw that the man was not merely well enough to leave the leper colony but was in fighting condition for the colony of heaven.

CHAPTER 10

And he arose out of the synagogue, and entered into Simon's house. And Simon's wife's mother was taken with a great fever; and they besought him for her. And he stood over her, and rebuked the fever; and it left her: and immediately she arose and ministered unto them.

LUKE 4:38-39 (ALSO MATTHEW 8:14-15; MARK 1:29-31),
KING JAMES VERSION

Among them was a woman who had suffered from haemorrhages for twelve years; and in spite of long treatment by doctors, on which she had spent all she had, there had been no improvement; on the contrary, she had grown worse. She had heard what people were saying about Jesus, so she came up from behind in the crowd and touched his cloak; for she said to herself, 'If I touch even his clothes, I shall be cured.' And there and then the source of her haemorrhages dried up and she knew in herself that she was cured of her trouble. At the same time Jesus, aware that power had gone out of him, turned round in the crowd and asked, 'Who touched my clothes?' His disciples said to him, 'You see the crowd pressing upon you and yet you ask, "Who touched me?" ' Meanwhile he was looking round to see who had done it. And the woman, trembling with fear when she grasped what had happened to her, came and fell at his feet and told him the whole truth. He said to her, 'My daughter, your faith has cured you. Go in peace, free for ever from this trouble.'

MARK 5:25-34 (ALSO MATTHEW 9:18-22; LUKE 8:43-48),
NEW ENGLISH BIBLE

One Sabbath he was teaching in a synagogue, and there was a woman there possessed by a spirit that had crippled her for eighteen years. She was bent double and quite unable to stand up straight. When Jesus saw her he called her and said, 'You are rid of your trouble.' Then he laid his hands on her, and at once she straightened up and began to praise God. But the president of the synagogue, indignant with Jesus for healing on the Sabbath, intervened and said to the congregation, 'There are six working-days: come and be cured on one of them, and not on the Sabbath.' The Lord gave him his answer: 'What hypocrites you are!' he said. 'Is there a single one of you who does not loose his ox or his donkey from the manger and take it out to water on the Sabbath? And here is this woman, a daughter of Abraham, who has been kept prisoner by Satan for eighteen long years: was it wrong for her to be freed from her bonds on the Sabbath?' At these words all his opponents were covered with confusion, while the mass of the people were delighted at all the wonderful things he was doing.

LUKE 13:10-17, NEW ENGLISH BIBLE

Peter's Mother-in-Law

The Woman Who Touched the Hem of

His Robe

The Hunchback

"ON LEAVING THE synagogue, he went to Simon's house." We find few clues to Jesus' living accommodations after He left home. He is almost never seen entering anyone's house. This incident is a rare exception. We have a gospel, not a diary of His private life, and the gospel goes on about what He did on the job, omitting His mailing address and the name of the places where He kept His things. We get the general impression that He and His disciples were roughing it. The New Testament life of Christ was transient, not domestic. It draws a picture of Jesus walking on the water, on the shore, from mountain to market place, any time of the day or night, sleeping or praying out under the stars as often as under the sun. But there is that tiny album of miniature portraits presenting Him practically as a member of the family of Mary and Martha; and here the evangelists hold Simon's house open an instant to give readers a glimpse of where Jesus went after church. Mark said it was "the house of Simon and Andrew" and saw Him entering with "James and John."

He chose these four important men first, and they had become friends as followers of John the Baptist. For a while, before Jesus filled any more apostolic places, He stayed with this nucleus at Peter's house down by the sea in Capernaum. They had been spending some exciting sabbath mornings together in synagogues; Jesus had only recently missed being murdered in His hometown, Nazareth. Jesus had been reading His favorite passage from Isaiah about His anointment: ". . . to preach the gospel to the poor; . . . to heal the broken-hearted, . . . and recovering of sight to the blind. . . ." The sermon had gone over extraordinarily well until He said, " 'Doubtless you will quote to me this proverb, "Physician, heal yourself" '. . . . And he said, . . . 'no prophet is acceptable in his own country. . . . there were many lepers in Israel in the time of the prophet Elisha; and none of them was cleansed, but only Naaman the Syrian.' When they heard this, all . . . were filled with wrath. . . . and put him out of the city, and led him to the brow of the hill, . . . that they might throw him down headlong. But passing through the midst of them he went away."

On another day, perhaps the following sabbath, "he went down to Capernaum. . . . And he was teaching them on the sabbath. . . ." By that time the disciples were almost afraid to go to the synagogue with Him and must have inaugurated the ancient custom of sitting as near the rear exit as possible. Then a madman went to pieces in the middle of Jesus' sermon and tried to break up the service; Jesus silenced him, though He had to save him to do it. But surprisingly, Simon's hometown treated Jesus well. The congregation was "amazed" and there were no ugly repercussions.

It must have been quite a relief to His men, for they seldom got any rest from threats and stones when worshiping with Jesus on the sabbath. But when they arrived home they found Peter's mother-in-law "in the grip of a high fever; and they asked him to help her." Apparently Peter had not only already settled down with a wife but had her sick mother in his home too. (The diagnosis "great fever," as the King James Version renders it, gives Trench the idea that it was not some minor malady but a classification of major fevers on the order of typhus. Some scholars suggest an attack of malaria.) Everyone seemed solicitous and anxious for Jesus to do something for the old woman, as He had helped someone at church. Had Peter's mother-in-law resented the invasion of Jesus into their privacy so much that matters had come to a head in the fever? Was her illness a sign that she wanted more attention from God, or yearned to be reconciled to a new way of life, or wanted to be reassured personally that despite her age everything was going to be all right ultimately?

Who cared about an old woman in those days? Women were illiterate, second-rate property, and at the mercy of whoever was head of the house. It was chivalrous for the gospel writers to introduce any women at all; ancient literature usually brushed them aside as some inferior beings who ate whatever bread the men left. Luke underlined Jesus' originality in honoring women—treating them as human beings belonged in the Good News—and many Marys are prominent in Luke, for Jesus' sake. It is very fitting that one of Jesus' first patients was that least of all women, a man's mother-in-law. No wonder women held Him higher and dearer, and were more faithful in the end.

Each evangelist describes the remedy differently. Matthew says that Jesus "touched her hand," Dr. Luke reports that the Great Physician "stood over her," and Mark, who never misses the action, mentions that "He . . . took her by the hand, and lifted her up." Luke adds that Jesus "rebuked the fever."

The consensus of opinion as to the result, however, is

unanimous: ". . . and immediately the fever left her, and she ministered unto them." We still do not understand why we have to get sick, why microbes are available, and what determines their success. Modern medicine is still working on the physical surface, plugging holes and stopping symptoms. According to the reports, Jesus went to the bottom of a woman's illness without the benefit of an X ray. He did not even insinuate that sin had a hand in it. He simply objected to the fever and overpowered it. He was not a diagnostician; He was good for her.

As far as we know, Jesus never had so much as a sore throat, and apparently He had a healthful effect on His intimates. The only one of His friends who got sick was Lazarus, and that happened in Jesus' absence and was corrected by His presence. Peter's mother-in-law was not sick when Jesus left that morning, but she improved rapidly as soon as He reappeared. That "she ministered unto them" on the sabbath sounds illegal but Jesus was shaking everyone's routine. "At a later time, the Rabbis forbade women to serve at the table, but probably Galilean peasants had no such scruples."

"So the news spread . . ." like wildfire and by sundown, when Jews were safe from sabbath regulations, Peter's doorway was jammed with sick people. Jesus' night's work was cut out for Him and He couldn't break away for prayer till daybreak. Healing was hard on Him, for His practice mushroomed and His privacy melted faster after each cure.

The woman who touched the hem of His garment is mentioned along with the raising of Jairus' daughter in three gospels. These two miracles intertwined immediately after the storm at sea and the storm in the breast of Legion. Jesus was on His way to the house of the president of the synagogue, possibly the same agreeable synagogue previously interrupted by the madman. That was an unexpected honor, considering the usual treatment Jesus received at the hands of such officials. The mission was not merely for a very important person; it was an emergency—the president's little twelve-year-old daughter was dying.

While Jesus was in a race with death for that little girl, a nobody interrupted Him. It was "a woman who had suffered from haemorrhages for twelve years. . . ." Hers was a chronic and obviously a very embarrassing complaint. "The affliction was a continuous uterine discharge. The woman is named 'Bernice' in Chapter 7 of the Greek MSS of The Acts of Pilate, and 'Veronica' in the Latin versions."

Mark adds something Dr. Luke doesn't care to dwell on: ". . . and in spite of long treatment by doctors, on which she had spent all she had, there had been no improvement; on the contrary, she had grown worse." She had gone downhill from doctor to doctor; every remedy had backfired and she had gone bankrupt paying for them. She was one of those embarrassing patients whose pain perversely refuses to respond to treatment. Was that trail of blood a symptom of some disease of the spirit? Was a broken spirit wreaking havoc on her organs, and was her sickness the spirit's way of sending out its SOS? Psychosomatic medicine doesn't cover every case, but every illness has more meaning than a simple matter of Vitamin K, sutures, and a bandage box. Illness can say something in another tongue and it might not hurt to ask, "What caused the cause of it?"

The woman had heard what people were saying about Jesus, so she "came behind him, and touched the hem of his garment: For she said within herself, If I may but touch his garment, I shall be whole."

Matthew and Luke are more explicit. It was *the fringe* that she *touched*. A *cicîth* or "sacred tassel" was tied by a blue thread to each of the four corners of the outer *garment* (Num. 15:38-39; Deut. 22:12)—a cloak that served as clothing by day and as a blanket by night. Such tassels were intended to remind Israelites of their obligations to the law, and are still affixed to the prayer shawl (the tallith) worn by orthodox Jews. The loose end of the cloak would have hung over Jesus' left shoulder, and the *cicíth* attached to it could have been touched by one who *came up behind him*—perhaps because she was ceremonially unclean. For other references by Luke to cure by contact see Acts 19:12.

She might have been superstitious or desperate, but not greedy. She didn't want to bother Him nor contaminate Him. All she wanted was to be near enough to feel the edge of His robe that dragged in the dirt. Her gesture was quite an expression of confidence for all its sentimentality, but we remember her doing it because it got results. All at once Jesus was within reach and suddenly she reached out, "And there and then the source of her haemorrhages dried up and she knew in herself that she was cured of her trouble."

Christ had "presence," and everything was so right with Him that it affected whatever was wrong with anyone else. Mind exerts far more control over bodily functions than we realize. A speaker's eloquence can make our tear ducts produce a saline solution. Embarrassment can bring the blood up the back of our neck and into our ears. Fear can produce goosebumps. Anger shoots adrenalin into the system, multiplying a man's strength and energy into a fury of its former self. What can love do to flesh and blood? Heaven knows, for few men love without ulterior motives. Jesus was one Man who actually cared enough whether we lived or died to go without eating, without sleeping, and down to the jagged gates of death without a "murmuring word." No one could touch Him without feeling the difference. "Bernice" said she noticed it immediately; it clotted the blood and reversed disintegrating forces inside her.

Jesus felt something, too: "At the same time Jesus, aware

that power had gone out of him, turned round in the crowd and asked, 'Who touched my clothes?'" The disciples were no different from us. What a ridiculous thing to ask, they thought, squeezed as they were in a twisting torrent of the population. "Meanwhile he was looking round to see who had done it. And the woman, trembling with fear when she had grasped what had happened to her, came and fell at his feet and told him the whole truth."

Whatever had been tearing her apart was now lying harmless in His hands. He wanted her to know that He did not object; the grace was not stolen but given with His compliments. The only Man to help her in twelve years was not found until she reached penniless desperation. Despite the appearances, there on the bottom of despair is a good place to look for rock. As usual, Jesus gave her confidence the credit; then He dismissed her with the traditional Semitic benediction among friends: "Go in peace. . . ." As He said goodbye, He added one more act of thoughtfulness—the blessed reassurance that her hemorrhage would never come back.

Eusebius said (*Ecclesiastical History*, VII.18) that there was "a statue, or rather two statues, in brass, one of Christ, another of this woman kneeling to him, which existed in his time at Caesarea Paneas, and which, according to tradition, had been raised by her in thankful commemoration of her healing." Legend or not, it does not seem such a strange thing for her to have done.

"One Sabbath he was teaching in a synagogue, and there was a woman there possessed by a spirit that had crippled her for eighteen years. She was bent double and quite unable to stand up straight." In that awkward position she probably could not even see Jesus to ask for help. And, no doubt, looking at the ground for eighteen years had dashed to pieces all her hopes of ever stretching up again. So, though she heard Him teaching, it did not occur to her to ask for anything for herself. She did not use her aching back as an excuse to stay home from church. There she was, apparently not bitter about it but sweet enough with faith to carry on with no complaints. But it broke Jesus' heart to see her, and He "called to her . . . , 'You are rid of your trouble.' " Apparently she gave Him her complete attention, which was a rare thing for people to do in those days—even these days. Somehow, with that cooperation from her, He was able to strike the chord that tied her down. Was it arthritic or hysterical? We only know He worked fast, packing a little more into His less-than-three-year ministry than most men could accomplish in several million lifetimes. The whole incident took only a few seconds. "Then he laid his hands on her, and at once she straightened up and began to praise God."

Christ's cures were never long-drawn-out, complicated ventures in radical surgery, requiring rows of knives, staffs of experts, and months of convalescence. He went straight to the heart of sickness, without the violence or necessity of exploratory operations.

He never seemed to be in a hurry during what we might call an emergency. Our flashing red lights and life-squad sirens would not have made any sense to Him. When Lazarus died, and when that little twelve-year-old girl was dying, He acted as though He had all the time in the world. Time was not of the essence to Him—God was. He did not allow latecomers to the fellowship of pain to push Him, but seemed to go first to sufferers with seniority; where they were concerned, He didn't put them off, even on the sabbath. His point of view made one president of a synagogue angry and another glad. But you cannot please everybody if you please God.

CHAPTER 11

And as Jesus passed on from there, two blind men followed him, crying aloud, "Have mercy on us, Son of David." When he entered the house, the blind men came to him; and Jesus said to them, "Do you believe that I am able to do this?" They said to him, "Yes, Lord." Then he touched their eyes, saying, "According to your faith be it done to you." And their eyes were opened. And Jesus sternly charged them, "See that no one knows it." But they went away and spread his fame through all that district.

MATTHEW 9:27-31, REVISED STANDARD VERSION

And they came to Bethsaida. And some people brought to him a blind man, and begged him to touch him. And he took the blind man by the hand, and led him out of the village; and when he had spit on his eyes and laid his hands upon him, he asked him, "Do you see anything?" And he looked up and said, "I see men; but they look like trees, walking." Then again he laid his hands upon his eyes; and he looked intently and was restored, and saw everything clearly. And he sent him away to his home, saying, "Do not even enter the village."

MARK 8:22-26, REVISED STANDARD VERSION

And they came to Jericho; and as he was leaving Jericho with his disciples and a great multitude, Bartimaeus, a blind beggar, the son of Timaeus, was sitting by the roadside. And when he heard that it was Jesus of Nazareth, he began to cry out and say, "Jesus, Son of David, have mercy on me!" And many rebuked him, telling him to be silent; but he cried out all the more, "Son of David, have mercy on me!" And Jesus stopped and said, "Call him." And they called the blind man, saying to him, "Take heart; rise, he is calling you." And throwing off his mantle he sprang up and came to Jesus. And Jesus said to him, "What do you want me to do for you?" And the blind man said to him, "Master, let me receive my sight." And Jesus said to him, "Go your way; your faith has made you well." And immediately he received his sight and followed him on the way.

MARK 10:46-52 (ALSO MATTHEW 20:29-34; LUKE 18:35-43),
REVISED STANDARD VERSION

As he passed by, he saw a man blind from his birth. And his disciples asked him, "Rabbi, who sinned, this man or his parents, that he was born blind?" Jesus answered, "It was not that this man sinned, or his parents, but that the works of God might be made manifest in him. We must work the works of him who sent me, while it is day; night comes, when no one can work. As long as I am in the world, I am the light of the world." As he said this, he spat on the ground and made clay of the spittle and anointed the man's eyes with the clay, saying to him, "Go, wash in the pool of Siloam" (which means Sent). So he went and washed and came back seeing. The neighbors and those who had seen him before as a beggar, said, "Is not this the man who used to sit and beg?" Some said, "It is he"; others said "No, but he is like him." He said, "I am the man." They said to him, "Then how were your eyes opened?" He answered, "The man called Jesus made clay and anointed my eyes and said to me, 'Go to Siloam and wash'; so I went and washed and received my sight." They said to him, "Where is he?" He said, "I do not know."

They brought to the Pharisees the man who had formerly been blind. Now it was a sabbath day when Jesus made the clay and opened his eyes. The Pharisees again asked him how he had received his sight. And he said to them, "He put clay on my eyes, and I washed, and I see." Some of the Pharisees said,

"This man is not from God, for he does not keep the sabbath." But others said, "How can a man who is a sinner do such signs?" There was a division among them. So they again said to the blind man, "What do you say about him, since he has opened your eyes?" He said, "He is a prophet."

The Jews did not believe that he had been blind and had received his sight, until they called the parents of the man who had received his sight, and asked them, "Is this your son, who you say was born blind? How then does he now see?" His parents answered, "We know that this is our son, and that he was born blind; but how he now sees we do not know, nor do we know who opened his eyes. Ask him; he is of age, he will speak for himself." His parents said this because they feared the Jews, for the Jews had already agreed that if any one should confess him to be Christ, he was to be put out of the synagogue. Therefore his parents said, "He is of age, ask him."

So for the second time they called the man who had been blind, and said to him, "Give God the praise; we know that this man is a sinner." He answered, "Whether he is a sinner, I do not know; one thing I know, that though I was blind, now I see." They said to him, "What did he do to you? How did he open your eyes?" He answered them, "I have told you already, and you would not listen. Why do you want to hear it again? Do you too want to become his disciples?" And they reviled him, saying, "You are his disciple, but we are disciples of Moses. We know that God has spoken to Moses, but as for this man, we do not know where he comes from." The man answered, "Why, this is a marvel! You do not know where he comes from, and yet he opened my eyes. We know that God does not listen to sinners, but if any one is a worshiper of God and does his will, God listens to him. Never since the world began has it been heard that any one opened the eyes of a man born blind. If this man were not from God, he could do nothing." They answered him, "You were born in utter sin, and would you teach us?" And they cast him out.

Jesus heard that they had cast him out, and having found him he said, "Do you believe in the Son of man?" He answered, "And who is he, sir, that I may believe in him?" Jesus said to him, "You have seen him, and it is he who speaks to you." He said, "Lord, I believe"; and he worshiped him. Jesus said, "For judgment I came into this world, that those who do not see may see, and that those who see may become blind." Some of the Pharisees near him heard this, and they said to him, "Are we also blind?" Jesus said to them, "If you were blind, you would have no guilt; but now that you say, 'We see,' your guilt remains."

JOHN 9:1-41, REVISED STANDARD VERSION

Two Blind Men

 The Blind Man of Bethsaida

Bartimaeus

 The Man Born Blind

ONE OF GOD'S good ideas was to get some light on creation and then to pass out to each person a pair of tiny windows so that everyone could see what he was doing. Who can fathom what a fairy tale it is to wake up in the morning with our own private eyes, two shining jewels to each man, to see for ourselves the dazzling splendor of day and night? Our eyes "open sesame" to stars dancing on black velvet, daffodils drifting in a sea of gold, falling petals of snow, the face of a child in prayer. Our other presents may seem small beside our sight. What right have we who see to grumble? When we weigh this ability, it tips our deficits the other way. What colors are yours, brown or blue?

A few people were missed. The tap-tap-tapping of their canes on the street beats into our ears, eats into our hearts. The world is bad enough with visibility. Not everything can be translated into ponderous Braille—blindness is a jail! Milton told us how hard it was behind those iron bars:

> . . . that one Talent which is death to hide,
> Lodg'd with me useless. . . .

The Near East was busy with blind men. It was a dust bowl of impurities that put out eyes with cataracts and trachoma. The long night in which so many lingered was one of the pressing reasons men looked for a Messiah who, among many other duties, was expected to make lame men walk and blind men see.

Jesus tried to keep this specialty a secret, and many cures were probably not recorded. These stories were so well guarded that each gospel is ignorant of its neighbor's news and has a different one to tell. Matthew alone remembers two that Jesus healed "indoors," presumably in the privacy of Peter's house. Mark remembers the time in Bethsaida when friends brought forth a blind man and Jesus "took the blind man by the hand and led him away out of the village" before He healed him.

Miracle working was bad publicity for a Saviour, since men uninterested in salvation might have misused Jesus for minor injuries. The New Testament maintains that miracles were not His major work but by-products of His loving power. The need of the hour was not twenty-twenty vision. What good was sight without something worth seeing? So Jesus' standard price for opening His patient's eyes was a promise that he would keep his mouth closed about it. Few sacrificed that much self-control to Jesus, and He was seldom paid. Not very many men can be trusted to do their part after their wishes come true; two of them "talked about him all over the country-side."

But almost all His patients were distinguished by their complete confidence in Him. At times their faith amazed Christ more than His miracles amazed them. As soon as His patients believed in Him, their affirmation of faith released

His power. Jesus made one concession to His blind patients: since He couldn't have eye-to-eye contact with them, the treatment always included a touch or the traditional use of clay and spittle. There was no stock prescription and each one was done a little differently.

One of the strangest features of Christ's miracles happened in His work with the blind: the blind man of Bethsaida had to have two treatments. His was the only problem in Jesus' practice that was not remedied at the first touch. Jesus "spat on his eyes, laid his hands upon him, and asked whether he could see anything. The man's sight began to come back, and he said, 'I see men; they look like trees, but they are walking about.' Jesus laid his hand on his eyes again; he looked hard, and now he was cured so that he saw everything clearly." Many eyes see men as trees; faces never come in focus and reality is blurred. How many of us are missing half the view? It takes two births to enter the Kingdom; perhaps all eyes must be opened a second time to see God.

Everybody knew about Bartimaeus. He was an institution who had begged his way for years at the gates of Jericho, taking ingenious advantage of everybody who passed by. Matthew said there was another blind man with him, and Luke thought Bartimaeus was blessed on their way into Jericho instead of on their way out, as Mark and Matthew remember it. Bartimaeus had good ears, "And when he heard that it was Jesus . . . he began to cry out. . . , 'Jesus, Son of David, have mercy on me!' And many rebuked him, telling him to be silent. . . ." Crowds are always shushing people. That one wanted to see Jesus, not to be bothered by a beggar. But Bartimaeus had a personality not easily squelched. He made his living by making noise; now he might get his eyes back, so "he cried out all the more. . . ." His voice interested Jesus far more than the crowd and He singled him out: "Call him." Suddenly Bartimaeus sensed with everything in him that his time had come, and impulsively, like a second Peter, "throwing off his mantle he sprang up and came to Jesus." Jesus must have been leaving Jericho, for there, in front of everybody, He violated His usual modesty.

Bartimaeus was a heart-breaker, a blind man whose spirit could not be broken. He would be remembered in that town for something better than beggary if God would only give him back his eyes. Jesus unmanned him with the question dearest to him: "What do you want me to do for you?" When Bartimaeus spoke, not saucily but pitifully eager, the words faltered under their load of hope and trust: "Master, let me receive my sight." The words were no sooner out than it was done, and Bartimaeus did a little better with his blessing than some others: he "followed him, glorifying God; and all the people, when they saw it, gave praise to God."

John headlined another story about a man born blind who was healed during the Feast of Tabernacles in Jerusalem. It came at the end of a long day of hot debate interrupted by the adulteress, and apparently on the sabbath day. This healing brought out the whole question of the origin of evil; it split the Pharisees and was the making of the patient himself. John found it to be a perfect illustration of Jesus as the Light of the world.

The patient did not come to Jesus until after his recovery. Jesus had picked him up after His disciples had pointed him out with the question: "Why was he born blind?" Jesus' answer is a volume on His attitude toward evil and illness in general. "'It is not that this man or his parents sinned,' Jesus answered; 'he was born blind that God's power might be displayed in curing him.'" This does not mean that God is the author of evil; He is, rather, its Eradicator. But in the process of removing evil, He has to use methods that will do the least harm and the most good. Lucifer is not God's agent but His spade. God takes advantage of all the harm the devil has done, and so, as Trench explains it, "willed that on this man should be concentrated more than the ordinary penalties of the world's universal sin, that a more than ordinary grace and glory might be revealed in their removing."

Jesus sealed the man's eyes with mud packs made of spittle and clay and prescribed, "Go wash in the pool of Siloam." (John defines Siloam as "Sent," just as Jesus was often defined.) A trip to a pool seems irrelevant, but perhaps a patient ought to be asked to do something to demonstrate his trust and humility. God communicates as we put a ring on a finger or get down on our knees; men can understand God best in the vocabulary of bread and wine; and so, Siloam was the sacrament of rebirth to a man who had been born blind.

The man opened his eyes amidst a cauldron of controversy over his Physician as Jews fought over the best way to fight the threat to their prestige. Never was a miracle done before a more skeptical audience. Some believed the patient was an imposter: ". . . it is someone like him." Pharisees asked him, and he verified his identity in vain. They tried to talk themselves and him out of such an awkward situation, but he would not be intimidated. Pharisees divided in two over it: some said a man of God would never do such a thing on the sabbath; others insisted no one else could have done it. The man born blind maddeningly insisted that Jesus was a prophet. After getting nowhere with the man, the Pharisees sent for his parents. The parents saw the light in the Pharisees' eyes and, since it was a grievous sin at that point to appreciate Jesus, they took what amounted to our Fifth Amendment and cowardly referred the prosecution to their son as Exhibit A.

"So for the second time they summoned the man who had been born blind, and said, 'Speak the truth before God. We know that this fellow is a sinner' " What they meant was:

"Tell us what we want to hear. We've decided, and if you know what's good for you, you'd better agree quickly!" But Jesus had picked a winner that time, and the man born blind would not be browbeaten. He would not admit that Jesus was a sinner and announced rather devastatingly, "All I know is this: once I was blind, now I can see." They tried to catch him up, but he was equal to their cunning and inquired, "Do you also want to become his disciples?"—which made them explode with abusiveness.

As soon as the Pharisees said, ". . . we do not know where he comes from," the man born blind grabbed the initiative and came into his own: "What an extraordinary thing! Here is a man who has opened my eyes, yet you do not know where he comes from! It is common knowledge that God does not listen to sinners; he listens to anyone who is devout and obeys his will. To open the eyes of a man born blind—it is unheard of since time began. If that man had not come from God he could have done nothing." He had destroyed their case, so "they expelled him from the synagogue."

When Jesus heard that the man had been excommunicated for witnessing, He looked him up and asked, " 'Do you believe in the Son of Man?' He answered, 'And who is he, sir, that I may believe in him?' Jesus said to him, '. . . it is he who speaks to you.' He said, 'Lord, I believe.' " That man saw not only the light of day, but the Light of the world.

"Some Pharisees in his company asked, 'Do you mean that we are blind?' 'If you were blind,' said Jesus, 'you would not be guilty, but because you say "We see", your guilt remains.' " God will be gentle to the blind and hardest on those who do not live up to the light they have. We must remember that there is a more important light than meets the eye—even blind, deaf, and dumb Helen Keller found it.

CHAPTER 12

He left the territory of Tyre again and passed through Sidon to the sea of Galilee, crossing the territory of Decapolis. And a deaf man who stammered was brought to him, with the request that he would lay his hand on him. So, taking him aside from the crowd by himself, he put his fingers into the man's ears, touched his tongue with saliva, and looking up to heaven with a deep sigh he said to him, "Ephphaha" (which means, Open!). Then his ears were at once opened and his tongue freed from its fetter—he began to speak correctly. Jesus forbade them to tell anyone about it, but the more he forbade them the more eagerly they made it public; they were astounded in the extreme, saying, "How splendidly he has done it all! He actually makes the deaf hear and the dumb speak!"

MARK 7:31-37, MOFFATT

Now when the supporters of Jesus saw what was going to happen, they said, "Lord, shall we strike with our swords?" One of them did strike the servant of the high priest, cutting off his right ear; but Jesus said, "No more of that!" and cured him by touching his ear.

LUKE 22:49-51 (ALSO MATTHEW 26:51-53; MARK 14:47-48; JOHN 18:10-11), MOFFATT

The Deaf Stammerer

Replacing the Ear of Malchus

MATTHEW MERELY MENTIONS that after Jesus returned from His trip to Tyre and Sidon, "Great crowds came to him, bringing with them the lame, the maimed, the blind, the dumb. . . ." But Mark goes into detail about the only deaf man in the gospels. He was not quite dumb; as we shall see in a later chapter, Matthew does introduce a dumb demoniac, but this is Mark's turn: "They brought to him a man who was deaf and had an impediment in his speech, with the request that he would lay his hand on him." To make it sacred, and perhaps to save the man embarrassment, Jesus "took the man aside, away from the crowd. . . ." It was a special mark of favor. Perhaps the man would remember he was not helped at a meeting but in a holy place apart, as if he were important to God alone. A deaf man might appreciate an action that spoke so loudly of His loving care.

Blindness, of course, is a tragedy, but we do the deaf an injustice to consider the loss of hearing simply a severe hardship. The silent world has its dark side, too. Communication is mankind's major invention so far, if it be fair to God to call it that. Speech is the obvious livery that displays our reason for being different from the brute, and the loss of hearing and speech is the unsung drawback to this development. It is no small shame for men to die with all their music in them. Part of a man has never lived if he has never heard "Happy Birthday to *You*," or has never made himself a joyful sounding noise unto the Lord. Think of the frustration of being forever muffled; the insult of being excluded from every conversation; of never being in on what is going on, except as an afterthought. How unfair it is to the other senses if one or two are dead.

Deafness is a symbol of far more than decibels can measure. Somehow man's ears got away from God since Eden, and our attention strays today from what He would like to say to us. Sounds can be a distraction; a man might as well be stone-deaf if he does not know how to listen for "the still small voice." As Dr. Herbert Lockyer notices, deafness to heaven soon betrays itself through a serious impediment in our speech. There is a dullness, a drab monotony in the tone of the voice of a man who misses the melody of the Kingdom. The life goes out of a man's vocabulary, religious words lose their luster, and the vibrance goes out of the hymns of him who has ceased to hear the Word of God.

Jesus' approach to the deaf man was an artistic visual aid— everything He did spoke to one who could not hear. He took him aside and gave him His complete attention. The deaf man could see Him "sigh," and "looking up to heaven" was not lost on him. When Jesus "put his fingers into his ears, spat, and touched his tongue," the man could see that Jesus wanted him to get well. Everything said that Jesus' heart was in the right place—but we say that phrase too superficially. It was because Jesus' heart belonged to God that His power was at the man's disposal. When someone's heart is in the right place, the results are explosive to the five senses; they burst the deaf man's ears open. Christ's love was like molten steel. Have we forgotten how well it stood up on the cross, went through hell, and came back after death? This Physician did not identify with a school of medicine, but with God.

The only thing Jesus could not do was to keep people quiet. They all noticed something about Christ's work that day that men fail to see about Christianity now: "All that he does, he does well." The church is still known for its charity, but not for its competence. It is time we returned to our Teacher for that next lesson, so that we may become known not simply as those who go about doing good, but as those who do it well.

We remember Gethsemane as the place where Christ prayed and was arrested. We forget that He also found time there to do one last miracle before His death. It happened after Judas arrived with the police. It was the only recorded time Christ healed someone who had been hurt in an act of violence. In Gethsemane Christ offered His services without request to rectify a wound inflicted by one of His own men.

According to Mark, an unnamed follower of Jesus struck off an ear of an unnamed slave of the high priest. Matthew (26:52-54) expands the account with a rebuke to the disciple. Luke identifies the severed member as the *right ear*, declares that Jesus *touched it* and *healed* the slave, and intercalates another version of Jesus' rebuke. In the Gospel of John (18:10-11), the disciple becomes Simon Peter, the slave Malchus, the ear the right one, and the rebuke still another saying, but there is no suggestion that any miracle was performed.

The problems of grafting on an ear are not as great as a few years ago. No doctor would be laughed at today for making the attempt. The unbelievable miracle is that Jesus had the presence of mind to look for that missing ear in the grass at Gethsemane, and that He had the thoughtfulness to put it back where it belonged. Peter's mistake seemed mighty small beside the one Judas and the police were making. Who cares about someone's ear at a time that makes all the difference in the world? Jesus cared, and on His way to the cross He stooped down to pick up someone's ear and put it back.

Anyone who saw that could see that He was not negotiating

from weakness. Peter's violence smacks of defensiveness done in desperation. But Jesus did not retreat to the cross: "Do you think that I cannot appeal to my Father, and he will at once send me more than twelve legions of angels?" Jesus was going to the cross because He wanted to—for God. The crown could easily have been His, but He took the cross so that the Scriptures might be fulfilled, and men like Malchus and you and me might not be mutilated but saved. Now we know how right He was, for the cup He drank covers the earth in blessing in a way we would never have known if He had fought with the sword.

CHAPTER 13

When he entered Capharnahum again, after some days, it was reported that he was at home, and a large number at once gathered, till there was no more room for them, not even at the door. He was speaking the word to them, when a paralytic was brought to him; four men carried him, and as they could not get near Jesus on account of the crowd, they tore up the roof under which he stood, and through the opening they lowered the pallet on which the paralytic lay. When Jesus saw their faith, he said to the paralytic, "My son, your sins are forgiven." Now there were some scribes sitting there who argued in their hearts, "What does the man mean by talking like this? It is blasphemy! Who can forgive sins, who but God alone?" Conscious at once that they were arguing to themselves in this way, Jesus asked them, "Why do you argue thus in your hearts? Which is the easier thing, to tell the paralytic, 'Your sins are forgiven,' or to tell him, 'Rise, lift your pallet, and go'? But to let you see that the Son of man has power on earth to forgive sins"—he said to the paralytic, "Rise, I tell you, lift your pallet, and go home." And he rose, lifted his pallet at once, and went off before them all; at this they were all amazed and they glorified God saying, "We never saw the like of it!"

MARK 2:1-12 (ALSO MATTHEW 9:1-8; LUKE 5:17-26), MOFFATT

After he had ended all his sayings in the hearing of the people he entered Capernaum. Now a centurion had a slave who was dear to him, who was sick and at the point of death. When he heard of Jesus, he sent to him elders of the Jews, asking him to come and heal his slave. And when they came to Jesus, they besought him earnestly, saying, "He is worthy to have you do this for him, for he loves our nation, and he built us our synagogue." And Jesus went with them. When he was not far from the house, the centurion sent friends to him, saying to him, "Lord, do not trouble yourself, for I am not worthy to have you come under my roof; therefore I did not presume to come to you. But say the word, and let my servant be healed. For I am a man set under authority, with soldiers under me: and I say to one, 'Go,' and he goes; and to another, 'Come,' and he comes; and to my slave, 'Do this,' and he does it." When Jesus heard this he marveled at him, and turned and said to the multitude that followed him, "I tell you, not even in Israel have I found such faith." And when those who had been sent returned to the house, they found the slave well.

LUKE 7:1-10 (ALSO MATTHEW 8:5-13), REVISED STANDARD VERSION

So Jesus came again into Cana of Galilee, where he made the water wine. And there was a certain nobleman, whose son was sick at Capernaum. When he heard that Jesus was come out of Judaea into Galilee, he went unto him, and besought him that he would come down, and heal his son: for he was at the point of death. Then said Jesus unto him, Except ye see signs and wonders, ye will not believe. The nobleman saith unto him, Sir, come down ere my child die. Jesus saith unto him, Go thy way; thy son liveth. And the man believed the word that Jesus had spoken unto him, and he went his way. And as he was now going down, his servants met him, and told him, saying, Thy son liveth. Then enquired he of them the hour when he began to amend. And they said unto him, Yesterday at the seventh hour the fever left him. So the father knew that it was at the same hour, in the which Jesus said unto him, Thy son liveth: and himself believed, and his whole house. This is again the second miracle that Jesus did, when he was come out of Judaea into Galilee.

JOHN 4:46-54, KING JAMES VERSION

The Paralytic

The Centurion's Servant

The Nobleman's Son

THERE IS NO rush for ringside seats in church today. Doesn't Jesus come any more? Now it takes seven days to scrape up enough people for a service. In Jesus' time a crowd swarmed simply on a rumor that He was back in town—and His audiences were not men who thought they'd better come to make up for the month they'd missed. Those crowds came for more pressing reasons. Christ asked good questions, but so did Socrates. Men came because Jesus had the answers to the very things that were killing them. We might presume that only a precious few peers of genius could possibly appreciate the Master of them all; but no, the main army of His listeners was drawn from the scrap-heap of heartbreak. No doubt the curious were included, but His assemblies were always distinguished by the arrival of the desperate. Men did not come to Him calmly to pass the time or discuss the problems of the day, but breathlessly, pitifully, through their tears, to pray, "Master, help me."

One particular time "He was speaking the word to them, when a paralytic was brought to him; four men carried him, and as they could not get near Jesus on account of the crowd, they tore up the roof under which he stood, and through the opening they lowered the pallet on which the paralytic lay." The patient might have been a young man, for Jesus said "son." Whatever was wrong, he couldn't move a muscle and had to be carried in.

This miracle is a compliment to four forgotten men who went far beyond the line of duty. They remind us that the miracles of Christ demand that others take the initiative and supply the sacrifice. This event meant teamwork; a Good Samaritan could not have carried it off single-handedly. Some pilgrims are too paralyzed to undertake the Christian adventure, and their mental block cannot be broken except from outside. How many miracles in other men must wait until we interfere with their inertia and drag them bodily to the feet of Christ? We must not sink to button-holing and strong-arming, but neither can we go to sleep and let the devil pick men off so easily.

The four men probably did not have to bring the patient against his will. Perhaps they told him the gospel truth in such a way as to win his willingness for one last try. It has been done—enthusiasm is infectious. Every step they took might have given hope another breath. Perhaps their moral support had him saying before he got there:

> You bring me news
> Of a door that opens at the end of a corridor,
> Sunlight and singing; when I had felt sure
> That every corridor only led to another,
> Or to a blank wall.

Faith often is so fragile that it looks for the slightest excuse to give up. Fair-weather Christians are frightened away at the first sign of rain and Sunday mornings are at the mercy of any other alternative. The faith of these four men was more virile; it was not bull-headed and argumentative but indefatigably bright. When they saw that the house was packed and the doorway jammed, they didn't start a fight or stop in self-pity. They simply had another inspiration; and I think their flair for originality came from the fact that they simply could not believe that the four of them could not get through to Christ. The typical reaction of Christians outside a crowded church door is often a relieved "We'll-try-it-again-next-Sunday." They rationalize their half-heartedness away as the courteous thing to do, but their quick retreat is a confession that they don't really care. But a good businessman will swim through a flood if his deal depends on it, and this four-man committee adopted a similar approach to God. They defied the door, tore through the clay-covered saplings of Peter's roof, and lowered their burden of grief down through the opening to get the Master's attention. Faith found the opening doubt would never have guessed was there. These men made clear forever afterward that faith is something more than a stab in the right direction; it is a determined invasion. A miracle takes more than a breath of faith, and their mission was accomplished only after faith received its second wind.

How did Jesus react to such a novel interruption of His sermon? How upsetting these acrobatics would be to our formality of worship! Who would dare delay the Sunday-morning march of the minister's deathless prose after the bulletins had already been printed as a safeguard against spontaneity? Probably the best the contemporary clergyman could do, and still keep his dignity, would be to signal the ushers and call to anybody clawing through the roof, "You boys come down from there and come in the door as you're supposed to!" A modern minister might object to a lot of dust and clay coming down on his freshly-laundered regalia. Unless, as Luke (being a foreigner to Palestine) leads us to believe, Peter had the only tiled roof in Capernaum, it would have been a risk to look up at the baked clay crumbling in the resolute hands of the invaders.

Apparently, Jesus exulted in the sign of life overhead. He immediately assumed, not that the devil had disturbed the peace, but rather that God had dropped a man in His lap for help. He was flexible enough to be equal to any change of pace and He was neither flustered nor angered, but fascinated, by the four men looking down who had providentially given Him a marvelous opportunity to perform a miracle. No doubt He assumed God had decided the meeting needed some improvement at that very moment. The men had done their part to make the worship service exciting and memorable—He would do His.

"My son, your sins are forgiven." The convict of guilt was pardoned on the basis of his friends' credentials. But did Jesus tease that poor stick of a man with a seemingly irrelevant announcement? It is irrelevant to us only. Men recognized in those days a relationship between sin and sickness; at least Jesus sensed that the man was suffering more from shame than muscle failure. Illness hurt more in those days because physical disability was an exposure of unrighteousness. Forgiveness did not seem at all secondary to those casualties thirsting for God's favor first. Doubtless the paralytic was more excited about having his soul set than about walking again. So was Jesus. A perfect physical cure is never permanent; He could guarantee spiritual healing only.

But that was blasphemy. Only God could forgive sins. Who did Jesus think He was? The righteous indignation of the Pharisees mounted rapidly to the point of murder. And so, almost as an afterthought to confirm His right to speak for God, Jesus went on to add, "Rise, I tell you, lift your pallet, and go home." That visible show of power was convincing, and silently they let the stones slip out of their hands as they stood aside to let an obviously innocent invalid walk home under his own power. They couldn't kill anybody after that. Did the four men forget to repair the damaged roof or did poor Peter have to patch it up himself? The story ends by saying, ". . . at this they were all amazed and they glorified God saying, 'We never saw the like of it!' "

Another miracle showed off the faith of a man, making Jesus Himself gasp in amazement, and wrung from Him the finest compliment He ever paid a foreigner. There was a Roman garrison stationed in Capernaum, presumably numbering about one hundred men. Its commanding officer was called a centurion and while he was a noncommissioned officer in the custom of the empire, his authority was comparable to that of our captain. We can assume that a man holding that position had some learning and culture, and was not unaware of his exclusive privileges as a Roman citizen and the unquestioned authority owed him by everyone as the hand that held the emperor's mace in Galilee.

This particular centurion was a very special person who "had a slave who was dear to him, who was sick and at the point of death." Commentators cannot agree whether his attachment was emotional or economic; I think there is no question of his human interest. According to Luke, "When he heard of Jesus, he sent to him elders of the Jews, asking him to come and heal his slave." The fact that even the Jews could think of something good to say about the centurion inclines us to a very high opinion of him. He was no rough military boss of a remote post. He was not merely solicitous in bothering to call a doctor for his slave. His messengers, who were very important leaders of the nation under him, volunteered this reference: "He is worthy to have you do this for him, for he loves our nation, and he built us our synagogue." He does not sound at all like his superior, Herod, who was head over Palestine. Here was one philanthropist who was not resented. And, of course, "Jesus went with them."

According to Luke, as Jesus neared army headquarters, the centurion sent out friends to stress his humility, but Matthew claims that the centurion came in person to meet Jesus "As he entered Capernaum. . . ." Since Matthew ought to know, Capernaum being his hometown, let us allow him to introduce the supporting star. Matthew makes the dialogue more direct and dramatic: " 'Sir,' " said the centurion, " 'a boy of mine lies at home paralysed and racked with pain.' Jesus said, 'I will come and cure him.' But the centurion replied, 'Sir, who am I to have you under my roof? You need only say the word and the boy will be cured. I know, for I am myself under orders, with soldiers under me. I say to one, "Go," and he goes; to another, "Come here," and he comes; and to my servant, "Do this," and he does it.' " The military man respected the chain of command. His men minded him, and he knew that all the boy needed to get rid of his spasm was a word from the divine Tribune. He was a man who kept his word, and so it was not hard for him to believe that God would keep His. It was one of the few occasions in His life when Jesus was staggered; not even His disciples had ever expressed so much confidence in Him. Christ, who had prayed for Peter to have faith, was stunned to see it shining in this good soldier's eyes. "Jesus heard him with astonishment. . . ."

Then Jesus said, "I tell you this"—and I think He was searching for words worthy enough to decorate the heroism of the man's devotion—"nowhere, even in Israel, have I found such faith." We make a mistake if we marvel at the miracle more than the centurion's burst of confidence. He helped Jesus get over the humiliation in His hometown where He could do "not many mighty works because of their unbelief." At a time like this we can almost see what Christ could do if He had a little boost of belief from us who profess so much but would never dare to lay it on the line in public as that alien did.

Somehow the centurion had learned his lesson well in another school of discipline. He had developed an eye for judging men. He knew whom to salute and, by experience on the field of battle, who could be trusted with authority. What this world needs today is a few talent scouts who can find, in all the masquerading, just where the Messiah is. That centurion spotted the Son of God in remote Galilee, and everything in his military experience told him instinctively that here was a Man before whom Caesar himself should fall down. He grasped the fact that still proves so elusive—that God Himself had delegated all authority, dominion, and power here incarnate, and that one little word from Him would dismiss so small a thing as sickness at any distance. Some of us may not think as highly of Christ, but we should at least revere in memory the faith of a Roman centurion who honestly treated Jesus as if He were the King of kings. Then, in fairness, we should pause to remember that there was, as far as we know, no report that the centurion was ever disillusioned after what Jesus said to him: " 'Go home now; because of your faith, so let it be.' At that moment the boy recovered."

Some scholars assume that "The Nobleman's Son" is John's version of "The Centurion's Servant." "It would almost seem as if Irenaeus had thought so; and some in the time of Chrysostom identified the two miracles; who himself, however, properly rejects this rolling up of the two narratives into one. By Ewald too this identification is taken for granted, though without the smallest attempt at proof." Bishop Trench argues convincingly that the story of the nobleman's son is not a repetition of the story of the centurion's son. Anyone can easily tell the two stories apart. John's story is about the son of a Jewish nobleman sick with paralysis in Cana; Matthew and Luke tell about the slave of a heathen centurion bedridden with a fever in Capernaum. In Cana Jesus was asked to come and refused; in Capernaum He was asked not to come, even though He volunteered to go. In "The Centurion's Servant," Jesus meets a man of great faith; in "The Nobleman's Son," Jesus makes a man of faith. Jesus had complete confidence in the centurion's motives but questioned the nobleman's.

Perhaps the most significant distinction between the two stories is the use of faith. The centurion's faith came first and the miracle grew out of it. The reverse is true in the case of the nobleman; with him the miracle came first and his faith afterward. The miracle came as a reward to the centurion's faith, but was the reason for the nobleman's. The second story shows that faith can be reversible, and that gave John a good reason to include it in his gospel. The stories are similar in describing the intercession of one man for another, and healing at a distance with a word; but they are strongly individual in expressing the facility of the Master's use of faith.

CHAPTER 14

When they came back to the disciples they saw a large crowd surrounding them and lawyers arguing with them. As soon as they saw Jesus the whole crowd were overcome with awe, and they ran forward to welcome him. He asked them, 'What is this argument about?' A man in the crowd spoke up: 'Master, I brought my son to you. He is possessed by a spirit which makes him speechless. Whenever it attacks him, it dashes him to the ground, and he foams at the mouth, grinds his teeth, and goes rigid. I asked your disciples to cast it out, but they failed.' Jesus answered: 'What an unbelieving and perverse generation! How long shall I be with you? How long must I endure you? Bring him to me.' So they brought the boy to him; and as soon as the spirit saw him it threw the boy into convulsions, and he fell on the ground and rolled about foaming at the mouth. Jesus asked his father, 'How long has he been like this?' 'From childhood,' he replied; 'often it has tried to make an end of him by throwing him into the fire or into water. But if it is at all possible for you, take pity upon us and help us.' 'If it is possible!' said Jesus. 'Everything is possible to one who has faith.' 'I have faith,' cried the boy's father; 'help me where faith falls short.' Jesus saw then that the crowd was closing in upon them, so he rebuked the unclean spirit. 'Deaf and dumb spirit,' he said, 'I command you, come out of him and never go back!' After crying aloud and racking him fiercely, it came out; and the boy looked like a corpse; in fact, many said, 'He is dead.' But Jesus took his hand and raised him to his feet, and he stood up.

Then Jesus went indoors, and his disciples asked him privately,

'Why could not we cast it out?' He said, 'There is no means of casting out this sort but prayer.'

MARK 9:14-29 (ALSO MATTHEW 17:14-20; LUKE 9:37-43),
NEW ENGLISH BIBLE

The Epileptic Boy

ALL THREE SYNOPTICS tell the only gospel story of epilepsy, but with slight variations. Mark and Luke consider it as a case of demon-possession, but all agree on the symptoms which clearly support Matthew's diagnosis of epilepsy. The King James Version renders epilepsy as "lunatick," meaning "moonstruck," the word coming from the Latin *lunar*, "moon." Ancients supposed that the affliction struck those who had sinned against the moon whose phases they believed governed the seizures.

"On the next day, when they had come down from the mountain, a great crowd met him." Mountain climbers might appreciate the epic peak that had just been reached. Jesus had led Peter, James, and John to the altitude of transfiguration. As a matter of fact, the crowd had already surrounded the rear guard of disciples who were left behind, and they were arguing with their backs to the wall against a slew of cunning lawyers. Apparently the height and burning weight of glory still shone in Jesus' face, for, according to Mark, the mere sight of Him broke up the argument: "As soon as they saw Jesus the whole crowd were overcome with awe, and they ran forward to welcome him." The scene is reminiscent of Moses' descent from Sinai, although then the people "were afraid to come nigh him," and Moses' mission was to punish. Jesus' appearance was magnetic and His first move was merciful.

Jesus immediately took command of the situation: " 'What is this argument about?' A man in the crowd spoke up: 'Master, I brought my son to you. He is possessed by a spirit which makes him speechless. Whenever it attacks him, it dashes him to the ground, and he foams at the mouth, grinds his teeth, and goes rigid.' " Raphael's painting points up the vast contrast and close connection between the Mount of Transfiguration and the epileptic fit in the valley below. The gospels move in a moment from God to the devil in this scene as Jesus came down off the roof of the world to break a boy out of the devil's basement.

"I asked your disciples to cast it out, but they failed." That is what a lot of people are saying about His disciples now. We are such incompetent, fumbling successors of the Master; we muff all the miracles He left us to do. Christians have had to surrender so many areas in which He shone. Who can see the resemblance between us and our Namesake? Most people who get sick or get into trouble now call a lawyer or a physician instead of contacting the disciples because of our sorry record of religious clumsiness and inexcusable "don't care-ness." Men do not bow down to confess any more—they lie down on couches. Think of the damage so-called disciples have done to His eminence in salvation. Will men have to bypass our church to get back to Christ? "I asked your disciples. . . , but they failed."

"Jesus answered, 'What an unbelieving and perverse generation!' " Is it any wonder He was wild with weariness for a minute, after having been above the clouds of distrust to see so clearly what could happen if men would only trust their Father in heaven? It would have been far more surprising if He had not been distressed at the difference between what He saw up there and down here.

" 'Bring him to me.' So they brought the boy to him; and as soon as the spirit saw him it threw the boy into convulsions, and he fell on the ground and rolled about foaming at the mouth." The flopping limbs and jerking spasms, the eyeballs rolled back, bring to mind the horror and despair of everyone who watches these hopeless and devastating seizures. Jesus immediately put Himself in the father's place, and with that heartfelt feeling for the right word so dear to the humiliated, He asked, "How long has he been like this?" The father knew immediately that He was Someone who appreciated the misery he had been through and gratefully spilled the heavy history he had borne for his son. " 'From childhood,' he replied; 'often it has tried to make an end of him by throwing him into the fire or into water. But if it is at all possible for you, take pity upon us and help us.' "

" 'If it is possible!' said Jesus. 'Everything is possible to one who has faith.' " There He goes again, shattering our neat and complicated calculations of mice and men. How can we be condescending to Someone so eminently and permanently successful? Jesus will be saying the same thing to men many centuries after our point of view will have passed out of style. What will men be saying then of our contemporary attitude toward any show of strength in Scripture? Sydney Lanier confessed:

> O age that half believ'st thou half believ'st,
> Half doubt'st the substance of thine own half doubt,
> And, half perceiving that thou half perceiv'st,
> Stand'st at thy temple door, heart in, head out!

But someone, sooner or later, is going to have enough nerve, enough need to break the chain of skeptic conformity and church lethargy and take Christ at His Word. The defeated father had reached that point. He decided it was about time to quit monkeying with alternate sterile pretensions and become God's guinea pig. So he made a prayer any agnostic might make if he suddenly decided to come down from his defiant high horse. He was honest enough to admit that he had doubts, and humble enough to indicate they hadn't done much good. In fact, he seemed ashamed of his suspicious nature and was eager to believe he could be wrong. "I believe," he cried, "help thou mine unbelief."

A miracle was made from a man's request for faith. God knows we're human; no one can help having doubts. But we are not asked to have perfect faith to start with. All we need to move a mountain is a grain of faith in place of that grain of salt we've been using. Salt is dead, but a grain of faith will grow. Surely, that father's faith did not stop with a grain. Socrates always said, "Be reasonable," and we look back to him for logic. But the world isn't getting anywhere with logic, as we can see. The One we look up to encouraged us to have faith. Why don't we try that?

"'Deaf and dumb spirit,' he said, 'I command you, come out of him and never go back!'" Epileptic fits come and go, but Jesus was dismissing the disease, not simply one seizure. In the truest sense of the word, Christ had a *wholesome* effect on the lad. Whatever lack of electric discipline or birthmark on the brain had been bringing on the convulsions, it went out at His command.

"Why could not we cast it out?" When did the disciples last cure an epileptic? It was so long ago we can't remember. A whole world of disbelief has gotten in our way and eclipsed His talent for healing. Doctors are doing fairly well controlling epilepsy with medicine now. Is that what God means for us to do? Should the church abdicate all further responsibility for meddling in healing? If suffering were being solved, we might say "yes." But the planet is still a snake pit of misery and the most brilliant surgery still looks hit-and-miss compared to His radiant effect.

What is it that makes some teachers good disciplinarians? There is something about them that gets cooperation and affection as well as prompt obedience from a student who, in another class, tries to get away with murder. There are generals who have the gift for giving an order in a way that fires the imagination of their men. There was something about King David that made two volunteers risk their lives to get him a drink of water. We cannot plumb the depths of Christ's nature, but there was something so commanding about His slightest wish that it elicited a total response from the whole person. Everything leaped to attention when He spoke. A man was most himself and never felt better than in His presence. He had an effect that penetrated to the center of an epileptic boy's nervous system; it was not a feat of medicine.

"There is no means of casting out this sort but prayer."

But RSV is correct in omitting *and fasting*, with several of the best MSS. This omission is justified on the following grounds: (a) Jesus did not practice fasting (2:19); (b) Matt. 17:20 gives an entirely different answer, apparently from Q (but cf. Mark 11:22-23); (c) Matt. 17:21 is a gloss, which has in turn provided the καί νηστεία in some MSS of Mark. But even without "fasting," Jesus' answer is surprising. Jesus is represented in Mark as the Son of God, whose power over the demons is immediate and irresistible; yet here he states that prayer is the secret of successful exorcism! If we had asked Mark the question, he would probably have replied that the answer was meant for the disciples, and for the later church: "*You* cannot cast out this kind of demon save by prayer." At the same time, we may well see in these words an authentic record of Jesus' own view of his extraordinary healing power; *by prayer* means not a momentary ejaculation, but a life of intimacy with God through personal communion (cf. 1:35; 6:46, and even the strange and distant echo in John 11:41-42).

THE MIRACLES OF CHRIST

·III·

The
Healing
of the Mind

CHAPTER 15

He was driving out a devil which was dumb; and when the devil had come out, the dumb man began to speak. The people were astonished, but some of them said, 'It is by Beelzebub prince of devils that he drives the devils out.' Others, by way of a test, demanded of him a sign from heaven. But he knew what was in their minds, and said, 'Every kingdom divided against itself goes to ruin, and a divided household falls. Equally if Satan is divided against himself, how can his kingdom stand?—since, as you would have it, I drive out the devils by Beelzebub. If it is by Beelzebub that I cast out devils, by whom do your own people drive them out? If this is your argument, they themselves will refute you. But if it is by the finger of God that I drive out the devils, then be sure the kingdom of God has already come upon you.

'When a strong man fully armed is on guard over his castle his possessions are safe. But when someone stronger comes upon him and overpowers him, he carries off the arms and armour on which the man had relied and divides the plunder.

'He who is not with me is against me, and he who does not gather with me scatters.

'When an unclean spirit comes out of a man it wanders over the deserts seeking a resting-place; and finding none, it says, "I will go back to the home I left." So it returns and finds the house swept clean, and tidy. Off it goes and collects seven other spirits more wicked than itself, and they all come in and settle down; and in the end the man's plight is worse than before.'

LUKE 11:14-26 (ALSO MARK 3:22-30; MATTHEW 12:22-32; MATTHEW 9:32-34), NEW ENGLISH BIBLE

The Controversial Exorcism

"HE WAS DRIVING out a devil . . ."—that was not out of character for the Son of God. The gospels give us four colorful scenes showing Jesus in action as an Exorcist, and they indicate He did that kind of work often, as the Messiah was supposed to do.

Both Mark and Luke identified Matthew's case of epilepsy as demon-possession. Perhaps it should be said in their defense "that in essence hysteria and epilepsy are not fundamentally different, that the course of the disease is the same, but is manifest in a diverse form in different intensity and permanence. Epilepsy, Walshe adds, has no morbid anatomy that has yet been discovered with the resources at our disposal."

The ancients believed in spirits and took them seriously as an explanation for anything. Stones, trees, and men were very accessible homes for infestations of amoral demons from the unseen world. We have had our witch hunts and we still have our nightmares. In those days, a man never knew when he might wake up as another man, or not quite himself, because some outsider had broken in during the night and taken over his self-control.

The New Testament idea of demonology was far ahead of its time—perhaps ahead of our time. There, demonic activity was always a diabolical part of the devil's conspiracy. Demons were superhuman, not supernatural, footmen of Satan who found their way into a vulnerable host and brought excruciating conflict to reason and morality. The gospel is completely innocent of the rash of exotic and obsolete data typically associated with the subject in the medieval as well as the ancient world. The three or four cases selected for the canon are noteworthy for their artistic restraint and modern relevance.

According to Scripture, God is not a dual personality playing chess against Himself—one hand moving white men, the other black. He is at war with the nether kingdom set up by the treasonous will of Satan; and for some reason that finite mind cannot fathom, God will not use main force to extinguish "the devil and his angels" but restricts Himself to the good weapons of righteousness and truth. We mortals live in a pinch between two worlds; as good comes down, evil comes up from below. Luther sang in Scriptural terms:

> And though this world, with devils filled,
> Should threaten to undo us;
> We will not fear, for God hath willed
> His truth to triumph through us.

This is what the writer of Ephesians meant when he said, ". . . we wrestle not against flesh and blood, but against principalities, against powers, against the rulers of the darkness of this world. . . ."

The tortured spirits the New Testament presents are not done for; the raging conflict and state of frenzy today suggest that the battle is not over. The stone-dead sinner is a smooth operator who quietly submitted to Satan's control long ago. Peter said to Ananias, ". . . why hath Satan filled thine heart to lie to the Holy Ghost. . . ?" John attempted to explain Judas: ". . . the devil having now put into the heart of Judas . . . to betray him."

Having a demon is probably the unhappiest situation, but

not the guiltiest. The existence of Satan does not exonerate Eve from all responsibility. Satan teases, but Adam and Eve have to agree to it. Screwtape can't get in to take over if someone doesn't leave the gate open. Mental illness is also a moral issue, although only God knows who deserves the blame along with the poor victim. But there comes a time in the descent or disintegration of any man when he is no longer responsible for his action. He is at the mercy of invading forces, manipulated by unleashed passions rampaging over the helpless conscience.

Contemporary Christians prize these precious few instances of demon-possession in the New Testament, for they vividly illustrate the extension of the struggle for morals and reason into the sphere of the unconscious. Correspondingly they demonstrate Christ's sovereignty in that grim no-man's land. We cannot neatly correlate our cases of paranoia and melancholia with the tormented examples brought before Jesus. However, "the term 'obsession' (Latin for siege) is sometimes used as equivalent to 'possession.'" Surely, some of the madmen hopelessly inhabiting the asylums of our century would look strangely familiar to the Authority who figured out and corrected some earlier disorders of personality.

One immediately admires Jesus' calmness and good sense when He was up against madness. The Great Physician would have nothing to do with the flourishing superstitions and prescribed fetishes of handwashing and dieting in which His most distinguished contemporaries were caught. He was free of the antics of the witch doctor and the magic of fads which have ranged from bloodletting to hormone injections. The medical practices of twenty years ago appear primitive beside today's; yet Jesus mysteriously managed to avoid falling into pitfalls that would have dated Him. His heart went out so successfully to the victims of insanity, who until recently were treated with every conceivable indignity and torture. When one recalls the ingenious cruelties mankind has traditionally inflicted on those thought to be afflicted with witches or demons—which turns the annals of medicine into a savage house of horrors—we are awed at the sensitivity and assurance with which Christ entered into that domain. What a blessed relief it is to come up out of the dark, crowded, and understaffed snake pits of our own day into the refreshing air the Galilean brought to this still sad affair. We do not dismiss current analysis and diagnosis as irrelevant, but they are somehow elementary beside the swiftly integrating force of faith that was ignited in the presence of the Master.

". . . and when the devil had come out, the dumb man began to speak." Certainly not all dumbness was caused by demons, although they could induce it as well as other physical malfunctions. One of Matthew's two versions of this case adds that the man was blind, but apparently the poor wretch's behavior gave him away as "possessed" rather than simply blind, deaf, and dumb.

"The people were astonished, but some of them said, 'It is by Beelzebub prince of devils that he drives the devils out.'" That charge was a grudging concession to Christ's therapeutic power; critics couldn't conceal the results, so they put the worst possible interpretation upon them. They would wipe Him and His wonders out one way or another. Mark mentions that "people were saying that he was out of his mind." "Later enemies said Christ learned his tricks from an Egyptian juggler, a charge that Celsus adopted and embellished. He pictured an Orthodox Jew addressing Christ scornfully: 'You cured diseases. . . ; you restored dead bodies to life; you fed multitudes with a few loaves. These are the common tricks of the Egyptian wizards, which you may see performed every day in our markets for a few half-pence.'" As Christ's effectiveness increased, the charges against Him became more menacing, until finally He was smeared by association with a devil: "*Beelzebub* is derived from the Hebrew text of II Kings 1:2-3, where Baalzebub ('lord of flies') is a contemptuous perversion of Baalzebul ('lord of the temple'), the name of the god of Ekron. But *Beelzebul* in Aramaic was open to the derogatory interpretation 'lord of dung.' None of the forms has been found in Jewish literature as a name for Satan."

Jesus did not descend to mudslinging; He answered the real questions His antagonists have raised in other's minds. The devil could quote Scripture and work wonders to support himself, but by definition the devil could not do anything good without helping God. Jesus deftly defended His miracles from this scandal: "Every kingdom divided against itself goes to ruin, and a divided household falls. Equally if Satan is divided against himself, how can his kingdom stand?—since, as you would have it, I drive out the devils by Beelzebub." Would Satan work through Christ to attack his own evil agents?

". . . by whom do your own people drive them out?" Respected Jews were reputed to have cast out devils. Clearly, they would not have cared for Jesus' interpretation of their powers. Jesus did not object to exorcism done by anyone; when a strange competitor upset His disciples, He said, ". . . he that is not against us is for us." But the occasional performance of miracles, both in the past and present, promised a crescendo of power as the Kingdom approached, and Jesus drew their attention to His extraordinary success as the sign of His fulfillment of that expectation: "But if it is by the finger of God that I drive out the devils, then be sure the kingdom of God has already come upon you."

"When a strong man fully armed is on guard over his castle his possessions are safe. But when someone stronger comes upon him and overpowers him, he carries off the arms and armour on which the man had relied and divides the plunder." "In Mark and in Matthew the 'strong man' of this parable is a householder, and the situation contemplated is one of violent robbery. In Luke the *strong man* is a prince whose *palace* is captured by armed assault. In both forms the one point is that Satan is now impotent. Allegory not only identifies Jesus with the *one stronger than he,* but also Satan's human victims with *his goods* and *his spoils* and the demons with *his armor.*"

"He who is not with me is against. . . ." ("Jesus declares that the kingdom of God is set over against the kingdom of Satan, and that there is no place for neutrals in the conflict.") Then, in Luke, Jesus adds "a warning to demoniacs who have been cured to guard against the danger of relapse. More probably it is a parable." It is not enough "When an unclean spirit comes out of a man. . . ." ". . . a new dynamic must replace the old tyranny. To express it in Paul's phraseology, the faithful must be the temple of God and the dwelling place of God's Spirit (I Cor. 3:16)."

"Anyone who speaks a word against the Son of Man will receive forgiveness; but for him who slanders the Holy Spirit there will be no forgiveness." Luke delays this passage until a little later, but both Matthew and Mark agree that it follows the parable of the strong man. Despite the confusing controversy over the meaning of the unforgivable blasphemy against the Holy Spirit, it becomes clearest in connection with the "Beelzebub controversy," as Frederick Grant explains:

> . . . every sin and blasphemy will be forgiven except blasphemy against the Holy Spirit; this cannot be forgiven, because, some theologians say, the blasphemer is incapable of repentance. The one who so blasphemes, attributing the work of God's Spirit to Satan, or to human self-interest, *is guilty of an eternal sin* (not KJV, *in danger of eternal* damnation); . . . The passage is one that has given rise to endless speculation regarding 'the unforgivable sin'. . . . It is safe to say, theologically, that certainly very few persons have ever been guilty of this "unforgivable" sin. Few have ever said with Milton's Satan, "Evil, be thou my good." At the same time, the danger of it is constant—the attribution

of divine works of mercy and restoration to human personal ambition, to mercenary or political aims, to lust for power, or to collusion with the powers of darkness. . . . the accusation brought against Jesus by the scribes no doubt implied their guilt, as it also implied that of others who repeated the slander.

CHAPTER 16

And they went into Capernaum; and immediately on the sabbath he entered the synagogue and taught. And they were astonished at his teaching, for he taught them as one who had authority, and not as the scribes. And immediately there was in their synagogue a man with an unclean spirit; and he cried out, "What have you to do with us, Jesus of Nazareth? Have you come to destroy us? I know who you are, the Holy One of God." But Jesus rebuked him, saying, "Be silent, and come out of him!" And the unclean spirit, convulsing him and crying with a loud voice, came out of him. And they were all amazed, so that they questioned among themselves, saying, "What is this? A new teaching! With authority he commands even the unclean spirits, and they obey him." And at once his fame spread everywhere throughout all the surrounding region of Galilee.

MARK 1:21-28 (ALSO LUKE 4:31-37), REVISED STANDARD VERSION

Jesus then left that place and withdrew to the region of Tyre and Sidon. And a Canaanite woman from those parts came crying out, 'Sir! have pity on me, Son of David; my daughter is tormented by a devil.' But he said not a word in reply. His disciples came and urged him: 'Send her away; see how she comes shouting after us.' Jesus replied, 'I was sent to the lost sheep of the house of Israel, and to them alone.' But the woman came and fell at his feet and cried, 'Help me, sir.' To this Jesus replied, 'It is not right to take the children's bread and throw it to the dogs.' 'True, sir,' she answered; 'and yet the dogs eat the scraps that fall from their masters' table.' Hearing this Jesus replied, 'Woman, what faith you have! Be it as you wish!' And from that moment her daughter was restored to health.

MATTHEW 15:21-28 (ALSO MARK 7:24-30), NEW ENGLISH BIBLE

The Demoniac in the Synagogue

The Daughter of the Syrophoenician Woman

"*AND THEY WENT* into Capernaum; and immediately on the sabbath he entered the synagogue. . . . And they were astonished at his teaching. . . . And immediately there was in their synagogue a man with an unclean spirit; and he cried out. . . ." That was the first time Jesus ever met a man who was "possessed," according to Mark, and so the occasion marks a highly dramatic moment in His ministry. Of course, it was only the first of many fantastic situations and spectacular successes that characterized His performance in Peter's hometown. Apparently the auspicious event took place in the synagogue built by the benevolences of the Roman centurion and presided over by Jairus, both of whom were soon to be coming to Jesus with requests as exciting and marvelous in themselves as the results they were to win through Him. He never knew what to expect in that community; it was the place where the roof opened up over His head to squeeze in one more miracle for Him to do, and where His sermon was so moving that He put an obsessed creature under compulsion.

What a strange place to find a demoniac—in church!—although some critics feel the devil is safest in that sleepy atmosphere. But Christ was God in Person and that conflicting current burned the rebel and made him yell. His reaction was defensive, desperate, but Jesus did not ignore the insulting mutiny nor wait in silence till the discourtesy was over. Immediately following up on His advantage, the One who spoke so gently to sinners addressed sin imperiously: "Silence!"—and the bluffing defiance obediently ran away. We still suffer from the havoc of evil, but the effective shout of Christ that day signaled the beginning of the end of the kingdom of Satan. The battle between good and evil is not over, but we Christians believe that the Best Man is on our side; it is only a question of time and faith.

"And Jesus . . . withdrew to the district of Tyre and Sidon." Trench insists that He never left home and that this phrase means He was on the edge of the country, not in the interior. While He was in the area, "a Canaanite woman from that region came out and cried, 'Have mercy on me, O Lord, Son of David; my daughter is severely possessed by a demon.' But he did not answer her a word." This was a most baffling breach of courtesy, if that is what it was. Of course, the woman was a foreigner—Mark calls her "a Greek, a Syrophoenician by birth." She could not have had a more antagonizing ancestry in the eyes of a good Jew. She was a checkered descendent of the original inhabitants of Canaan, the lowest breed of Gentile, one of Baal's illicit daughters. As a Phoenician, she was in the grip of the mother-goddess Ashtoreth, or Astarte, one of the most corrupting influences ever connected with religion, which required and counseled every form of vice and perversion in the name of piety.

Perhaps Jesus' silence came from the shock that a person with her background would ever think of coming to Him. Did the silence express discrimination? Apparently it drove her to His disciples, and when she made a nuisance of herself they begged Him to send her away. Why had He not already sent her away? Was He waiting for the will of God? No doubt He wondered how far His disciples' flexibility could stretch from Palestine. The heathen woman was outside His immediate responsibility and she was without the background of faith necessary for His miracles. No daughter of the opposition could receive such a blessing out of casual greed. Was she trying to exploit a visiting wizard? His silence was her examination; He would let her teach Him a lesson. Homer's lines unconsciously had Christ in mind:

> Persuasive speech, and more persuasive sighs,
> Silence that spoke, and eloquence of eyes.

He still did not send her away. "'I was sent,'" He told her, "'only to the lost sheep of the house of Israel.' But she came and knelt before him, saying, 'Lord, help me.'" He did not say "No." Why not? One easily recognizes here, on the growing edge of His role, that He was simply not able to refuse a genuine petition. How deeply was she concerned? How far would she trust? "And he answered, 'It is not fair to take the children's bread and throw it to the dogs.'" Was Jesus insulting her or exposing a chilling provincial point of view? Jesus certainly was not calling Gentiles "dogs" but was using the familiar aphorism of His time; and whether, as some scholars argue, the Greek word for "dogs" here can mean "pets," we cannot avoid the conclusion that the Man who was so quick to compliment the centurion, who appreciated the hated Samaritans, and characteristically showed particular kindness to defenseless women and little children, surely used this phrase gently, perhaps humorously, here, as a gracious Southerner might say "damnyankee." In any case, He spoke kindly enough to insure a spirited and resourceful reply: "Yes, Lord, yet even the dogs eat the crumbs that fall from their master's table." Even if Jesus had to regret His roughness, He was quick to make up for it and eager to praise her disarming victory in the contest of wits: "O woman, great is your faith! Be it done for you as you desire."

Why was it . . . Christ stayed long, wrestling with her faith, and shaking and trying it to see if it were sure-footed or no? Doubtless because he saw in it a faith which would stand the proof, knew that she would emerge victorious from the sore trial; and not only so, but with a mightier and purer faith than if she had borne away her blessing at once and merely for the asking. Now she has learned, as then she never could have learned, "that men ought always to pray and not to faint;" that when God delays a boon he does not therefore deny it. . . . She had won the strength which Jacob won from his wrestling til the day broke, with the angel. . . . There, as here, we note the same persevering refusal on the other; there, as here, the stronger is at last overcome by the weaker. God himself yields to the might of faith and prayer. . . . The angel of the convenant was no other than that Word, who, now incarnate, blest this woman at length; as he had blest at length Jacob at Peniel, in each case so rewarding a faith which had said, "I will not let thee go, except thou bless me."

We remember what a hopelessly debauched prodigal young Augustine was. Many parents would have relinquished such a son to hell, yet his mother absolutely refused to give up hope that he could become great in the sight of God. As he went from bad to worse she prayed day and night and knocked relentlessly on doors for help, from priest to bishop. Even the most heartbreaking news of his last escapade could not break her faith in his eventual salvation. Finally, the weary bishop concurred and wrote to her: "It is not possible," he said, "for the son of all these tears to perish." How right he was. How right she was. How right was the Syrophoenician mother to hang on until she won the admiration of Christ Himself and the glad news that "her daughter was healed instantly."

CHAPTER 17

So they reached the other side of the sea, and landed in the region of Gerasa. As soon as he got out of the boat, a man possessed by a foul spirit came out of the burial places near by to meet him. This man lived among the tombs, and no one could any longer secure him even with a chain, for he had often been fastened with fetters and chains and had snapped the chains and broken the fetters; and there was no one strong enough to master him, and night and day he was always shrieking among the tombs and on the hills and cutting himself with stones. And catching sight of Jesus in the distance he ran up and made obeisance to him and screamed out,

"What do you want of me, Jesus, son of the Most High God? In God's name, I implore you, do not torture me." For he was saying to him,

"You foul spirit, come out of this man."

He asked him, "What is your name?"

He said, "My name is Legion, for there are many of us."

And they begged him earnestly not to send them out of that country.

Now there was a great drove of pigs feeding there on the hillside. And they implored him, "Send us among the pigs, let us go into them."

So he gave them permission. And the foul spirits came out and went into the pigs, and the drove of about two thousand rushed over the steep bank into the sea, and were drowned. And the men who tended them ran away and spread the news in the town and in the country around, and the people came to see what had

happened. When they came to Jesus and found the demoniac sit-
ting quietly with his clothes on and in his right mind—the same
man who had been possessed by Legion—they were frightened.
And those who had seen it told them what had happened to the
demoniac, and all about the pigs. And they began to beg him to
leave their district. As he was getting into the boat, the man who
had been possessed begged to be allowed to go with him. And he
would not permit it, but said to him,

"Go home to your own people, and tell them all the Lord has
done for you and how he took pity on you." And he went off
and began to tell everybody in the Ten Towns all Jesus had done
for him; and they were all astonished.

MARK 5:1-20 (ALSO MATTHEW 8:28-34; LUKE 8:26-39), GOODSPEED

Legion

LEGION IS THE New Testament's last word on demon-possession. Legion is Samson gone berserk. Neither Euripides nor Tennessee Williams ever wound up such a whirlwind of fury into one character or found a way to let it out safely and constructively as this miniature epic managed to do. And, of course, no psychiatric institute has ever had the unique pleasure of seeing sanity descend again on someone so indelibly lost in psychosis as the demoniac from Khersa. The story is full of Scriptural eccentricities; yet if the modern reader will control his prejudices and watch the breath-taking collision between heaven and hell carefully, it "comes off" as reality and compels belief.

Jesus is not cast here as an ascetic Galilean sapling, mouthing ethical nothings into the drowning screech of our jets; He is a Man at whose iron command chaos came out immediately and plunged to the bottom of the sea. We who have lost this faith in God's grip on creation through His Son are they who have fallen prey to superstition.

Shortly after Jesus and His disciples narrowly escaped a harrowing storm at sea, "they came . . . into the country of the Gerasenes." This story taught Dickens and Stevenson something about how to hold dread over the reader. When we disembark from Peter's boat, we step into the pagan stamping-ground of insanity and we are about to visit the gospel's monster. The distinguished Leslie Weatherhead revisited the site of this haunted house of Scripture and established the graveyard mood for our ghost story:

> They reach the eastern shore of the lake at eventide. At this point a gully or *wadi*, which I have myself explored, runs down to the shore, and we can imagine Jesus and his men walking up it in the dusk. This is Gentile territory. At the top of the *wadi* is a place of tombs, which to the Jew is a devil-haunted region. Furthermore, pigs are feeding in a great herd on the *bluff* at the top of the *wadi*, and to the Jew they are unclean animals. On a blazing June morning in 1934 I found this place strangely uncanny, wierdly desolate. If it made that impression on a Western mind on a sunny June morning, after a peaceful voyage in a motor boat, we can imagine the effect produced on the minds of the superstitious disciples, who thought pigs were unclean and graveyards full of devils, in the dusk of the late evening as they landed on what to them was a foreign shore, after a terrifying voyage during which they had been almost drowned.

It was no place to stop unless one wished to beard the devil in his den. Jesus did. "As he stepped ashore," a demoniac (Matthew mentions two) rushed to Him from "out of the tombs, so fierce that no one could pass that way." "He could no longer be controlled; even chains were useless; he had often been fettered and chained up, but he had snapped his chains and broken the fetters. No one was strong enough to master him. And so, unceasingly, night and day, he would cry aloud among the tombs and on the hill-sides and cut himself with stones."

The sudden appearance of a panting psychopath must have frozen the disciples. Apparently even Peter was speechless. The man was not only mentally disturbed but criminally insane; he was at large only because bars and chains couldn't hold him. Presumably he charged, livid with rage, ready to live up to his bloodcurdling reputation for violence. None of the Synoptics forgot to tell us his impression.

"When he saw Jesus in the distance, he ran and flung himself down before him, shouting loudly, 'What do you want with me, Jesus, Son of the Most High God? In God's name do not torment me.' (For Jesus was already saying to him, 'Out, unclean spirit, come out of this man!')" Jesus acted as if emergencies were made for His miracles. Instead of paralyzing His power, the madman's offensive fired His conviction that absolutely nothing—not even a savage regiment of Satan— "can separate us from the love of God. . . ." The stunning thing about His manner was not simply His courage but His confidence. Already the demoniac was feeling the effects of an overwhelming force making him powerless. The defiance was not quite dead but he was already confessing and coming, like a little child, to Christ's feet.

"Jesus asked him, 'What is your name?'" A cynic might say, "What makes the difference?" But that was a big question in those days. "The very fact that Jesus asked the patient his name would be understood by the patient to mean that Jesus was seeking power over him by trying to understand the power that was controlling him. In the East to this day to surrender one's name to a person is to give that person power over one. . . . An Indian bride frequently will not give up her name to her bridegroom until after their marriage, when alone he has any rights or power over her. We remember that in the old Genesis story (32) the angel asks Jacob his name, and Jacob gives it. But when Jacob says to the angel, 'Tell me *thy* name,' no name is given. The angel had power over Jacob. Jacob had no power over the angel. Savages will rarely disclose their true names, for similar reasons."

" 'My name is Legion,' he said, 'there are so many of us.' "
" '*Legion*' was Latin for an army division of about six thousand, but the word had also been naturalized in Aramaic. According

to popular diagnosis, the severity of an affliction was proportionate to the number of demons who had caused it. . . ." Mary Magdalene was one "from whom seven demons had gone out. . . ." But this man housed an army of them.

Weatherhead suggests "that the word 'Legion' was a key to the origin of the shock which had brought on the illness."

In the First World War a man was found in no-man's land, wandering about between our trenches and those of the enemy, and the only word he could say was "Arras." This was the town in which he had been tortured to make him impart information, and the torture had driven him mad. Similarly, I remember the case of a man in a mental hospital during the First World War who had been tortured by the Germans, and the only word he would utter was the word "Boche." Here, in St. Mark's story, we have a man muttering the word "Legion," and it is not fanciful to suppose that he had suffered some shock at the hands of the Roman legion. We know from the story of the massacre of the innocents the kind of thing the Roman legion could do, and, indeed, it is possible that this patient had witnessed this dreadful affair. If he had seen tiny children slaughtered, and had rushed in from the sunny street terrified of the approaching soldiers whose swords were dripping red with blood, and had cried, "Mummy, Mummy, legion!" (if we may modernise his language), then it would be no flight of imagination to suppose that the childhood's shock—especially if the patient had a hereditary emotional unbalance—would be quite sufficient to drive him into psychosis. And now the community had exiled the patient right out of the security of their own fellowship into a wild graveyard in a foreign land, where he is left to live amongst the pigs, terrified by spasms of fear which leap up from his repressed memories into consciousness, and express themselves in maniacal frenzies and in loud cries.

"And he begged hard that Jesus would not send them out of the country. Now there happened to be a large herd of pigs feeding on the hill-side, and the spirits begged him, 'Send us among the pigs. . . .' " Who can explain this conversation adequately? We cannot separate the wild man's fancy from the terminology of the times, nor can we tell where Jesus' view began and the other left off. However, anyone who has ever tried to hold a conversation with a victim of delusions will not find this dialogue surprising. If the man interpreted his madness in such terms, there was nothing strange about his finding a solution to his predicament in a herd of pigs. We do not know enough to read between these lines but numerous possibilities present themselves to interpret the situation to our intellectual satisfaction. Animals are extremely sensitive to human emotions, and surely all the pent-up turbulence in Legion's breast—suddenly spilled—could have easily stampeded some hogs.

". . . and the herd, of about two thousand, rushed over the edge into the lake and were drowned." The story does not say that Jesus drowned the pigs. According to Thomas Aquinas, "That the swine were driven into the sea was no work of the divine miracle, but was the work of the demons by divine permission." We worry unnecessarily about the wasted pork. Artistically, the episode seems a very satisfying way to dramatize the extraordinary deliverance of Legion and the self-destructive destiny of the powers of evil. No matter how it happened, How much better is a man than a sheep?—or a pig?

"Furthermore, the patient and all his contemporaries believed that deep water is the only finally satisfactory way of getting rid of devils." According to Weatherhead, a sailor working on a ship at the waterline was said to be "between the devil and the deep blue sea" because it was believed that devils were dry-land creatures who didn't dare go near the water. Drowning is the devil's deadly enemy. We recall Jesus' story about the devil wandering through "waterless" places, and realize that a watery grave signified the extremity of punishment devils deserved; it was otherwise reserved for anyone who ever harmed "one of these little ones."

By far the most difficult feature of this miracle is man's usual failure to appreciate divine handiwork. After the pigkeepers had spread the word, people came in droves to find the pig farm deserted and "the madman . . . sitting there clothed and in his right mind; and they were afraid. . . . Then they begged Jesus to leave the district." The salvation of a madman seemed a small thing to the townspeople beside the loss of their precious property! We recognize in that human reaction that we are on genuine historical ground. We notice that there was no rejoicing because the terror of the tombs was silenced; everyone was too uneasy about the status quo of property to get excited about what had happened to a person. They apparently preferred insanity to any moral improvement that would cost so much. They regarded God as their enemy. Jesus ordered the devils to leave; then the townspeople asked Jesus to leave. How much of our own chattel would we surrender today if it would help a neglected neighbor get well? The rehabilitation of the ill and the excluded awaits the sacrifice by the well. If Christ will command the criminal spirits to leave, will we pay for it? Or will we too ask Christ to get out and leave us with our pigs?

"As he was stepping into the boat, the man who had been possessed begged to go with him." Modern pyschology might use the term "transference" to describe the vast shift that was taking place in the man's affections from graveyard ghosts to the Captain of the ship. Jesus refused him permission. He had not rescued the man to create an exhibit nor to exploit Him as a projection of His own personality. The belligerent hermit needed bracing social responsibility to recuperate. So the Physician, who had asked so many to keep His name secret, prescribed preaching for the man to keep him from falling back into his melancholy isolation. Legion needed to articulate his rescue over and over until it sank thoroughly into his unconscious and made up for the maturity he had missed during all those years of mental and moral confinement. Evangelism was therapy for him; and the witness of such a gentle Hercules must have won the wonder of those who knew him "back when." " 'Go home to your own folk and tell them what the Lord in his mercy has done for you.' The man went off and spread the news in the Ten Towns of all that Jesus had done for him; and they were all amazed."

Men have minimized the heroic epics in the gospels to devotional gossip and classified Christ with Professor Confucius. Legion, we *like* to say, was legend along with that whole list of alien anecdotes the evangelists left. But do you suppose our loss of memory betrays more cheap ingratitude than deep intelligence? Why do our minds draw a blank, become blocked when we try to think of something that would work us up to hero-worship? Disbelief in Christ's miracles is more to our discredit than His.

Let Legion live a minute. I like to think he walked away from that lightning stroke vowing that if he ever forgot what God had done for him he would be damned along with his devils. Time after blessed time the scarred and battered giant, who had been brought back from the dead, would bare his head; and with the light playing on his tear-streaked face, he would try to tell his listeners how beautiful life had become for him after Someone Else had wrenched hell's dirty hands off him and brought him safely home.

Let the desperate, forgotten rags of human beings lost and left for dead in the hygienic dungeons of our own swarming sanitariums remember Legion. Help them to forgive the church for snoring while they are jammed into hopelessness. May we yet somehow find the prerequisite faith to enable Christ to come and live in us so powerfully that in our epidemic of mental illness we may decipher the stirring example set for us the day the shackles fell from Legion and he was freed from a sea of meaninglessness.

The godless grunts and chilling roars on the moonlit shore, the sound of rattling chains in the morning fog are gone. One wild man was clothed and in his right mind because— we must remember—he first fell at the feet of Christ.

THE MIRACLES OF CHRIST

·IV·

The Raising of the Dead

CHAPTER 18

When Jesus had crossed again in the boat to the other side, a great crowd gathered about him as he stood on the shore. And a man named Jairus, the leader of a synagogue, came up and seeing him threw himself at his feet, and appealed to him, saying,

"My little daughter is at the point of death. Come, lay your hands on her, so that she may get well and live!"

So he went with him. And a great crowd followed him and pressed around him. . . .

Even as he spoke people came from the house of the leader of the synagogue and said,

"Your daughter is dead. Why should you trouble the Master any further?"

But Jesus paid no attention to what they said, but said to the leader of the synagogue, "Do not be afraid, just have faith."

He let no one go with him but Peter, James, and James's brother John. They came to the house of the leader of the synagogue, and there he found everything in confusion, and people weeping and wailing. And he went into the house and said to them,

"What is the meaning of all this confusion and crying? The child is not dead, she is asleep." And they laughed at him. But he drove them all out, and took the child's father and mother and the men who were with him and went into the room where the child was lying. And he grasped her hand and said to her,

"Taleitha, koum!"—that is to say, "Little girl, I tell you, get up!"

And the little girl immediately got up and walked about, for she was twelve years old. The moment they saw it they were *utterly amazed. And he strictly forbade them to let anyone know of it, and told them to give her something to eat.*

MARK 5:21-24, 35-43 (ALSO MATTHEW 9:18-26; LUKE 8:40-51),
GOODSPEED

The Daughter of Jairus

GOD WILL HAVE to multiply our shortage of faith by
some unkown quantity of infinity to get some people to
believe that Jesus ever did anything for the dead. It is hard
enough for them to swallow what He said; but to accept
the possibility that a perfect Stranger could resuscitate dead
bodies is going a little far for the students of Bertrand Rus-
sell. We ship all our corpses to the morgue, and we would
send for the men in little white coats if we heard that someone had sent for the minister for one last try after it was
too late.

Despite our failure in this advanced subject, the gospels
give us three examples of Jesus bringing the dead back to
life. The Man who was to be resurrected tried it on some
others first in a much more modest form. Of all people, the
first to give Christ the opportunity for this radical operation
was the distinguished president of the synagogue in Capernaum. As soon as Jesus had finished putting Legion back
together (perhaps it was during Levi's dinner for Him),
dignified Jairus came up and "threw himself down at his
feet and pleaded with him. 'My little daughter', he said,
'is at death's door. I beg you to come and lay your hands on
her to cure her and save her life.' So Jesus went with him. . . ."
But a hemorrhaging woman delayed Him and while He
was completing a miracle for her the president received the

dread news: "Your daughter is dead; why trouble the Rabbi further?"

That is a tragic point to reach. The time comes for so many people when they quit praying. They discover they can't have what they want and they don't go on to pray for what they should have. After their request has been denied, they don't want anything better. Since God won't play Santa Claus to their specifications, they assume He's stumped. Could it possibly be that God is not whipped by the circumstances that crush us and that He might like to share His secret to this new world if we would let go our petulance and play things His way? Perhaps our little scribble can be woven beautifully into the large design He's working on.

Death always makes a weak ending to a tragedy, but a child's death makes another act doubly demanding. Jesus hastened to say to Jairus, before his mind hardened in disillusionment, "Do not be afraid; only have faith."

We can't believe that Jesus was showing partiality to Jairus, but rather that He would have treated any bereaved father in this fashion—if the father had the flexibility and the childlike trust to turn to Christ at such a time. We miss the depth of meaning here if our faith stipulates that the child must return. Jesus' calmness exudes a confidence that God will come mightily and vividly to care for us and our little ones even in the presence of death if we will completely abandon our reservations and surrender ourselves to His mercy. Whether the child comes back to mortal life is not the issue. An even greater comfort comes if the assurance sweeps over the father of a dead child that she is safe from the perils of childhood and sitting happily and triumphantly in the lap of the perfect Father in heaven.

"They came to the president's house, where he found a great commotion, with loud crying and wailing. So he went in and said to them, 'Why this crying and commotion? The child is not dead: she is asleep.' But they only laughed at him." How can we call the Scriptures old-fashioned? Mockery of Christ is as modern as this minute. We think we are so enlightened if we have outgrown the antiquated embellishments of Holy Writ. Not at all!—the bystanders in Jairus' house beat us to doubt in His ability.

We do not mean to minimize the fantastic maturity it takes to believe that Jesus could do the impossible, but we Christians ought to recommend that cynics laugh at Him with a little more restraint—especially since the returns of life have not all come in yet. Suspicious as we are, no one has yet proven the gospels wrong nor given them much competition, though we've had two thousand years to try. Eugene O'Neill entitled a play *Lazarus Laughed*, partly because no emperor or society could scare the play's resurrected man into doing anything any more by holding death over his head. Let us laugh at Jesus a little less brassily lest the daughter of Jairus, the widow's son, and Lazarus have the last laugh on us.

"After this he allowed no one to accompany him except Peter and James and James's brother John. . . . After turning all the others out, he took the child's father and mother . . . and went in where the child was lying." The birthplace of a miracle has no room for scorn; first Jesus cleared out doubt. It makes us wonder what wonders might take place in the house of God now if all of those who no longer took Christ seriously were evacuated. Only a handful would be left, but that is all a miracle needed. Perhaps no great things will come from the church today until this prerequisite is filled; it is hard for faith to fight for its breath in the smug and stifling atmosphere of its enemy, arrogant disbelief, or, worst of all, that treasonous saboteur, pretending faith.

"Then, taking hold of her hand," He said to the child

in tender words which our gospels give us in the actual Aramaic that He spoke, "'Talitha cum', which means, 'Get up, my child.'" Strictly speaking, if we take Jesus' word for it, this particular child was not dead but perhaps in some deathlike coma which, without His interference, might have resulted in death. Years before, friends had requested Elisha to come and bring their boy back to life; so Elisha sent his servant Gehazi with his staff. That attempt by remote control failed, and not until the prophet arrived in person did the boy regain consciousness. And nothing happened in Jairus' house until Jesus entered and others left.

Trench has described it beautifully: "The house was now solitary and still. Two souls believing and hoping, stand like funeral tapers beside the couch of the dead maiden— the mother and the father. The church is represented in the three chiefs of its apostles." Jesus did the miracle without the impressive signs of showmanship that accompany the built-up stages of public faith-healers. The event was done effortlessly, in secrecy. "Immediately the girl got up and walked about—she was twelve years old." But Jesus was not an absent-minded expert of the other world. He understood children and was the first to think of saying, ". . . give her something to eat."

How did He do it? That knowledge is denied all except those who have *every* confidence in Him. Only the precious few who expect Him to be able to do what God alone can do may enter into the mystery of that inner sanctum.

CHAPTER 19

It was shortly afterwards that he made his way to a town called Nain, accompanied by his disciples and a large crowd. Just as he was near the gate of the town, there was a dead man being carried out; he was the only son of his mother, and she was a widow. Numbers from the town were with her. And when the Lord saw her, he felt pity for her and said to her, "Do not weep." Then he went forward and touched the bier; the bearers stopped. "Young man," he said, "I bid you rise." Then the corpse sat up and began to speak; and Jesus gave him back to his mother. All were seized with awe and glorified God. "A great prophet has appeared among us," they said; "God has visited his people." And this story of Jesus spread through the whole of Judaea and all the surrounding country.

LUKE 7:11-17, MOFFATT

The Widow's Son at Nain

"*IT WAS SHORTLY* afterwards that he made his way to a town called Nain, accompanied by his disciples and a large crowd." Trench has this to say in presenting the three miracles of the raising of the dead:

> They are not exactly the same miracle repeated three times over, but may be contemplated as in an ever ascending scale of difficulty, each a more marvelous outcoming of the great power of Christ than the preceding. For as the body of one freshly dead, from which life has just departed, is very different from a mummy, or a skeleton, or from the dry bones which the prophet saw in the valley of death (Ezek. XXXVI), so is it, though not in the same degree, different from a corpse, whence for some days the breath of life has fled. . . . Even science itself has arrived at the conjecture that the last echoes of life ring in the body much longer than is commonly supposed; that for a while it is full of the reminiscences of life.

The gospel, however, selects no mummies for its miracles. There are no puzzles of jumbled heads and odds and ends to be put back together. The evangelists did not believe everything they heard about Jesus, and we are struck by the contrast between their cautious selectivity and the coarse and artificial accounts offered in Apocryphal material. One is impressed with the literary agility of the evangelists which has stepped without stumbling into age after age, saying nothing that need offend the most scientific or the most sophisticated taste of our time. They seem to have catered much more to us than to their own contemporaries. Christ was the Lord of life; and if He were, as they insist, Lord over death, it is difficult to see how He could have worked these miracles—and they could have reported them—with greater sensitivity and intellectual elegance.

"Just as he was near the gate of the town, there was a dead man being carried out; he was the only son of his mother, and she was a widow. Numbers from the town were with her." This story shows Jesus in the act of doing something even the government would be afraid to do now—interrupting a funeral procession uninvited. Our first inclination is to retreat from such seemingly unhealthy behavior; but I think we cannot relinquish any of these last three stories as long as we hope to profess our Christian faith in the next world. If we, as Christians, believe in the resurrection of the dead—open though that may be to a vast variety of interpretations—we cannot afford to allow our first impression to erase these first three hints of that ultimate celebration. Of course we flounder helplessly in such deep waters. Who can make this much religion elementary?

As our Teacher reminds us, we cannot expect to have Christianity turn out right without the eventual destruction of our graves, which in some way is anticipated in these three preliminary events. Our Christian heritage insists that our spirits are not doomed to ethereal nakedness but shall, somehow in the providence of God, be housed in "incorruptible" substance. While these three dizzying exploits go beyond our minds' grasp, we maintain them at the distant upper edge of our comprehension as preparatory; for "immeasurably more stupendous than all these, will be the wonder of that hour, when all the dead of old. . . . shall be summoned from and shall leave their graves at the same quickening voice."

Luke is the only one who records Jesus raising the dead twice; no other gospel writer realizes what happened to the widow's boy at Nain. Nain is known for nothing else but this event; apparently it took place on the day after Jesus healed the centurion's slave. Fortified by that encouragement, Jesus traveled farther into faith on that tomorrow to turn tragedy upside down. Luke catches the sadness of the situation with two swift strokes of his pen: ". . . he was the only son of his mother, and she was a widow." It was too late to administer first-aid; but first-aid, last-aid, is merely makeshift. The most successful operation is only a stall for time and cannot stop the funeral procession from coming sooner or later.

But death seemed premature and thoughtlessly trespassing on the green lawn of a young man's life. It is a sin not to accept the inevitable. Earth is crowded with useless complaints and wasted resistance to the way things have to be, but perhaps we accept some things too quickly. It is a fine line, but many miracles were made from Jesus' refusal to adopt what we would normally call a healthy attitude of acceptance. "And when the Lord saw her, he felt pity for her and said to her, 'Do not weep.'" His compassionate words to that poor widow anticipate the promise God made to the rest of us in that parting remark of Scripture: "God shall wipe away all tears from their eyes; and there shall be no more death, neither sorrow, nor crying, neither shall there be any more pain. . . ." Jesus did not dispel the clouds of death for good; He broke through the clouds for an instant so that men could see the radiance shining brightly behind them.

"Then he went forward and touched the bier; the bearers stopped. 'Young man,' he said, 'I bid you rise.'" No words of ours could measure up to this extremity of action. Divinity is embarrassing to finite minds; such superiority makes us feel inferior. God has to go against the grain of our independence and self-reliance to be *for* us—which accounts, I think, for some of our mixed reactions to supernatural surprises. Those who are looking for Someone with a little longer reach—Someone who may know a little more about life and death than they do—might want to stop and look closely at the miracle at Nain: "Then the corpse sat up and began to speak; and Jesus gave him back to his mother." This is as far as faith will go. No man can see through Christ. All we can do is agree or disagree with what those present said: "God has visited his people." These last three miracles bring us to the door of heaven. Until it opens, "the rest is silence."

CHAPTER 20

There was a man named Lazarus who had fallen ill. His home was at Bethany, the village of Mary and her sister Martha. (This Mary, whose brother Lazarus had fallen ill, was the woman who anointed the Lord with ointment and wiped his feet with her hair.) The sisters sent a message to him: 'Sir, you should know that your friend lies ill.' When Jesus heard this he said, 'This sickness will not end in death; it has come for the glory of God, to bring glory to the Son of God.' And therefore, though he loved Martha and her sister and Lazarus, after hearing of his illness Jesus waited for two days in the place where he was.

After this, he said to his disciples, 'Let us go back to Judaea.' 'Rabbi,' his disciples said, 'it is not long since the Jews there were wanting to stone you. Are you going there again?' Jesus replied, 'Are there not twelve hours of daylight? Anyone can walk in daytime without stumbling, because he sees the light of this world. But if he walks after nightfall he stumbles, because the light fails him.'

After saying this he added, 'Our friend Lazarus has fallen asleep, but I shall go and wake him.' The disciples said, 'Master, if he has fallen asleep he will recover.' Jesus, however, had been speaking of his death, but they thought that he meant natural sleep. Then Jesus spoke out plainly: 'Lazarus is dead. I am glad not to have been there; it will be for your good and for the good of your faith. But let us go to him.' Thomas, called 'the Twin', said to his fellow-disciples, 'Let us also go, that we may die with him.'

On his arrival Jesus found that Lazarus had already been four days in the tomb. Bethany was just under two miles from Jerusalem, and many of the people had come from the city to Martha and Mary to condole with them on their brother's death. As soon as she heard that Jesus was on his way, Martha went to meet him, while Mary stayed at home.

Martha said to Jesus, 'If you had been here, sir, my brother would not have died. Even now I know that whatever you ask of God, God will grant you.' Jesus said, 'Your brother will rise again.' 'I know that he will rise again', said Martha, 'at the resurrection on the last day.' Jesus said, 'I am the resurrection and I am life. If a man has faith in me. even though he die, he shall come to life; and no one who is alive and has faith shall ever die. Do you believe this?' 'Lord, I do,' she answered; 'I now believe that you are the Messiah, the Son of God who was to come into the world.'

With these words she went to call her sister Mary, and taking her aside, she said, 'The Master is here; he is asking for you.' When Mary heard this she rose up quickly and went to him. Jesus had not yet reached the village, but was still at the place where Martha left him. The Jews who were in the house condoling with Mary, when they saw her start up and leave the house, went after her, for they supposed that she was going to the tomb to weep there.

So Mary came to the place where Jesus was. As soon as she caught sight of him she fell at his feet and said, 'O sir, if you had only been here my brother would not have died.' When Jesus saw her weeping and the Jews her companions weeping, he sighed heavily and was deeply moved. 'Where have you laid him?' he asked. They replied, 'Come and see, sir.' Jesus wept. The Jews said, 'How dearly he must have loved him!' But some of them said, 'Could not this man, who opened the blind man's eyes, have done something to keep Lazarus from dying?'

Jesus again sighed deeply; then he went over to the tomb. It was a cave, with a stone placed against it. Jesus said, 'Take away the stone.' Martha, the dead man's sister, said to him, 'Sir, by now there will be a stench; he has been there four days.' Jesus said, 'Did I not tell you that if you have faith you will see the glory of God?' So they removed the stone.

Then Jesus looked upwards and said, 'Father, I thank thee: thou hast heard me. I knew already that thou always hearest me, but I spoke for the sake of the people standing round, that they might believe that thou didst send me.'

Then he raised his voice in a great cry: 'Lazarus, come forth.' The dead man came out, his hands and feet swathed in linen bands, his face wrapped in a cloth. Jesus said, 'Loose him; let him go.'

Now many of the Jews who had come to visit Mary and had seen what Jesus did, put their faith in him. But some of them went off to the Pharisees and reported what he had done.

Thereupon the chief priests and the Pharisees convened a meeting of the Council. 'What action are we taking?' they said. 'This man is performing many signs. If we leave him alone like this the whole populace will believe in him. Then the Romans will come and sweep away our temple and our nation.' But one of them, Caiaphas, who was High Priest that year, said, 'You know nothing whatever; you do not use your judgement; it is more to your interest that one man should die for the people, than that the whole nation should be destroyed.' He did not say this of his own accord, but as the High Priest in office that year, he was prophesying that Jesus would die for the nation—die not for the nation alone but to gather together the scattered children of God. So from that day on they plotted his death.

Accordingly Jesus no longer went about publicly in Judaea, but left that region for the country bordering on the desert, and came to a town called Ephraim, where he stayed with his disciples.

JOHN 11, NEW ENGLISH BIBLE

Lazarus

THE RAISING of Lazarus is the masterpiece of all the miracles of Christ and by far the most expensive—it cost Him his life. This is John's seventh and final blow. At the first stroke, his Hero made wine flow from water at a wedding; at the last one, He made the blood run warm again in a man dead and buried in a tomb. It was the last straw for some of the mourners and they left to tattle to the authorities.

What more can a man say after Scripture has stunned him with an expedition into the other world? How does one approach Scripture's prize sensation? Is it going to be embarrassing? Will it be a blessing? Will we take it high and dry, like bookworms, without batting an eye? Are we buried so deep in unbelief that we will be as oblivious to the spectacle as the community of corpses among which Lazarus was laid to rest?

What do you do when someone robs a grave like that? It takes a good friend to stick by one till death, but Jesus crossed that great divide to go after Lazarus.

Surely, the scene should be cleared now of detractors and discreditors. Aren't our minds small enough already? We don't need any more men shrinking Scripture down to our size. The raising of Lazarus is at least more than a Rembrandt. Yet someone said, describing that old master's approach to this massive subject: "Rembrandt did everything he could to intensify the effect of this miracle." Why not make the attempt in words and see if we cannot come out of it better men than we were before—for Christ's sake, since He paid so dearly to do this for us?

The Bible allows only one gospel to handle the queen of His miracles. The other writers stand by in silence to let John tell the greatest wonder of them all. "There was a man named Lazarus who had fallen ill. His home was at Bethany, the village of Mary and her sister Martha." The sisters were already famous for being as different as night and day. Luke took us to their home before and introduced Martha as a person of "no nonsense" who complained about the way her sister was listening at Jesus' feet and not lifting a hand to help in the kitchen. Despite His preference for Mary's attitude on that occasion, Jesus played no favorites and soon found His way to the heart of bustling Martha. Now, it is brother Lazarus' turn to be the center of attention. His house was like a second home to Christ; it was the place He chose to spend His holiest week. It was where He slept on the last night He was able to get some sleep.

"The sisters sent a message to him: 'Sir, you should know that your friend lies ill.'" Jesus was often asked for help, but this special message came as a favor to Him. The news was forwarded as though He were next of kin and would want to know. Mutual trust and fondness shines in the absence of any request. John had confided in his previous chapter that Jesus had escaped from the police to John the Baptist's old place. The fact that the sisters knew where to find Him shows how close they were to Him.

It comes as a severe shock to discover that "after hearing of his illness Jesus waited for two days in the place where he was." If His tardiness puzzles us, imagine what it must have done to Mary and Martha. He was a day away. What went on in their minds as they watched Lazarus die and Jesus didn't come and didn't seem to care? There was no explanation, no excuse; it must have strained their relationship to the breaking point.

But that was the gentlest way for Jesus to set the stage for the maximum show of the glory of God. Jesus had to wait until every other help had failed, until the situation was absolutely hopeless. According to Jewish belief, the flesh did not begin to decay until the fourth day. So, "though he loved Martha and her sister and Lazarus," Jesus did not try to lift Lazarus until the fourth day after he had died. The restraint hurt Jesus too, for He said: "I am glad not to have been there . . ."—as if to confess He could never have put off His power and prolonged their agony had He been there.

"After this, he said to his disciples, 'Let us go back to Judaea.'" They couldn't believe their ears. That was the same as suicide—not bravery but utter absurdity! "The Jews down there are waiting to stone You on sight—that's why we left to come here!" So, when Jesus suggested that Lazarus only slept they insisted, ". . . he will recover"; and when He announced that Lazarus was dead they had even more reason to discourage the trip. But they couldn't talk sense into Him. He didn't seem to care if they all got killed, as long as He could view the dead body of Lazarus.

Jesus tried to soothe them with a proverb, assuring them that nothing could possibly hurt them before their time came. He didn't mean that life is like roulette, lasting until your number is up. Life lasts until God says it is ended. He meant that if the disciples flirted with danger doing the will of God, it would be no gamble. Everything was in God's hands—including them—and God would protect them on any errands He wanted them to run in the meantime. They led charmed lives as long as any portion of their daylight was left. The disciples heard Him speaking but what

He said was over their heads. He seemed determined to get them all murdered. So Thomas, seeing no other way out, sighed in self-pity: "Let us also go, that we may die with him." They went, but they were scarcely enthusiastic about the excursion. That miracle didn't get much support from the first disciples, either.

"As soon as she heard that Jesus was on his way, Martha went to meet him, while Mary stayed at home." Martha could not wait to ask, "Why? Why did you let us down?—let us lose Lazarus? Now it's too late." She had no breath for an exchange of pleasantries, no room in her heart for a welcome. Her first words broke over Him like an accusation: "If you had been here, sir, my brother would not have died." Mary was not even there to meet Him; she was somewhere else, lost in grief.

His disciples could not understand why He went back; His loved ones in Bethany could not understand what took Him so long. He tried to explain: "Your brother will rise again." Mourners seem to expect irrelevant platitudes from preachers at funerals, so Martha made more conversation: "I know . . . , at the resurrection on the last day." Suddenly she saw He was not fooling. There was something so compelling about the words as they came from *His* lips—they went through her like lightning. His whole manner was so commanding, His face so terribly beautiful, it struck her spirit to its knees. Their Physician had come too late, but in His place towered a Prince with power to act over life and death. The Man who stood before Martha had definitely not come to pay His respects. He had come back after Lazarus. Not even God Himself could deny this Son anything He asked. "Do you believe this?" He asked. From somewhere the words came: "'Lord, I do,' she answered; 'I now believe that you are . . . the Son of God. . . .'" Jesus raised Martha first.

On trembling legs and with wildly beating heart, Martha flew to Mary.

". . . and taking her aside, she said, 'The Master is here; he is asking for you.' When Mary heard this she rose up quickly and went to him." Jesus didn't go near the house but apparently went straight to the tomb upon arrival. That's where Martha met Him and where Mary headed. A funeral in those days was a three-day affront of tears and continuous wailing. "Bethany was just under two miles from Jerusalem," and since the family was well off and Lazarus was young, "many of the people had come from the city . . . to condole. . . ." Jesus avoided meeting the sisters under those cruel conditions. As soon as Martha whispered in her ear, Mary stole away to Jesus to get some peace. But the mourners saw her leave and followed, supposing she was going to the tomb to spill the paroxysm of her sorrow.

"So Mary came to the place where Jesus was. As soon as she caught sight of him she fell at his feet and said, "O sir, if you had only been here my brother would not have died." This is one of the most moving scenes in all literature; never was reproach so sweetly given. We ought, before we go any further with this miracle, to pause and marvel at Mary. Jesus was standing there—Mary fallen on the ground with hands outstretched—and her heart was in His hands. It was completely obvious to anyone who had eyes to see that He had done this to her, to her brother; yet she was at His feet worshiping the ground on which He walked—which is more than most mourners would do.

"Jesus wept." The sight of the crumpled, helpless girl, broken by her brother's death, brought to His mind the countless centuries that kind of thing had been going on: mothers saying goodbye to their sons for the last time; wives bidding farewell forever to the treasure of their hearts; tiny babies wilting at the breast; dazed fathers standing by as their own flesh and blood and bone were buried deep.

What do we feel when our earth's-eye view can't see above the horizon because life's tragedies have thrown us to the ground? Life seems to be one vast hoodwink, a cruel waste of time, leading to nothing. What is consciousness?— a meaningless hodgepodge of useless habits? Is mortality only a painful interval of beady-eyed dread until death breaks down the door and drags us off into the darkness?

"Jesus wept," and death met his match that day. ". . . he went over to the tomb. It was a cave, with a stone placed against it." If we are horrified now, we know exactly how everyone felt then. Martha couldn't bear the thought of Jesus going in the tomb, and begged, "Sir, by now there will be a stench; he has been there four days." She did not object because Jesus had risked His neck to return, but she could not allow Him to lose face forever among His friends. The last thing His followers wanted Him to do was to create a scene in the cemetery; He would never live down the scandal. The very idea—carrying on a conversation with a cadaver! But Jesus was immovable: " 'Did I not tell you that if you have faith you will see the glory of God?' So they removed the stone."

Mary and Martha would have been the first to agree with the disciples that living with Christ was never dull, and this time He outdid Himself. Martha could have died; the disciples were speechless, for a change. Mary's face was covered with her hands; no one moved a muscle. Jesus' first move still takes us by surprise: He stopped in the middle of all those people to tell God how much He appreciated His doing the resurrection for Him—as if it had already taken place!

Are we ready for the shock? Let's not be so quick to brace ourselves against it with mental seat belts safely fastened. The roof of modern belief may be built too low to hold all God would like to hand down. Let's remodel for this occasion; a shake-up might improve the mind.

In the graveyard were some people who couldn't even read.

This miracle was for them—and for us who have read too much. Jesus decided to do something we could see over the objections of too-scholarly scholars. Seeing is believing; so He raised His voice in a loud cry: "Lazarus, come forth." Jesus was not putting on an act for a pretty little stained-glass window; He was putting a soul and body back together. He was not reciting poetry for the demythologizers; His was an order to be obeyed.

No amount of (ministerial) spiritualizing ever gets through to people standing out in a cold dark graveyard. The only thing that makes sense is action; the only thing the weepers want is to have their loved one back.

I know of no one who is in a better position than John to tell us what happened that day in the graveyard; it is time we went to the primary source with a little more respect. There is no question in any reader's mind that John believed that Lazarus was raised, not in effigy but outright. The words reek with the vulgar smell of the tomb and explode with earthiness: "The dead man came out, his hands and feet swathed in linen bands, his face wrapped in a cloth." I don't think John took that spiritually—nor Martha, nor Lazarus, nor anyone else who was there.

No tests were made for brain damage. The same God who thought Lazarus up the first time had made him over. Actually, as Augustine noticed, resurrection must be easier for God than creation out of nothing. The most convincing proof of Lazarus' comeback, however, comes not from Jesus' friends but His enemies. Just as we expected (before their tears were dry), some of the mourners "went off to the Pharisees and reported" it.

The authorities took the raising of Lazarus rather seriously and Caiaphas met in emergency session with his council over the severe challenge to their leadership. Lazarus' second breath was "why the crowd went to meet him [Jesus] . . ."

when He entered Jerusalem. The last miracle not only made Palm Sunday but built the cross; for as John sighed, "So from that day on they plotted his death."

The raising of Lazarus was a promise of more to come. It meant not only the death of Christ but the beginning of the end of death, a prelude to a more sweeping experience. The two resurrections are intimately related through Mary. It was her love for Christ for raising Lazarus that led her to do a beautiful thing. Immediately after the upsetting funeral recorded in John, "a supper was given in his [Jesus'] honour, at which Martha served, and Lazarus sat among the guests with Jesus. Then Mary brought a pound of very costly perfume, . . . and anointed the feet of Jesus and wiped them with her hair, till the house was filled with the fragrance." Judas objected but Jesus said, ". . . she prepares for my burial. . . ." And so we say that the name of Lazarus was on the lips of Easter. The announcement was made right there to Martha: "I am the resurrection and the life."

BIBLIOGRAPHY

Augustine, *The City of God.*

Cairns, D. S., *The Faith That Rebels.* New York, Doubleday & Co., Inc., n.d.

Calvin, John, *Institutes.*

Farmer, H. H., *The World and God.* New York, Harper & Row, Publishers, 1935.

Gospel Parallels. New York, Thomas Nelson & Sons, 1957.

Kallas, James, *The Significance of the Synoptic Miracles.* Greenwich, Connecticut, Seabury Press, Inc., n.d.

Lewis, C. S., *Miracles.* New York, The Macmillan Company, 1947.

McCasland, S. V., *By the Finger of God.* New York, The Macmillan Company, 1960.

Pascal, Blaise, *Pensées, The Provincial Letters,* and *Scientific Treatises.*

The Interpreter's Bible, Vols. 7 and 8. Nashville, Abingdon Press, 1951 and 1952.

Trench, Richard C., *Notes on the Miracles of Our Lord.* Westwood, N. J., Fleming H. Revell Company, 1953.

Weatherhead, Leslie, *Psychology, Religion, and Healing.* Nashville, Abingdon Press, 1952.

Wendland, Johannes, *Miracles and Christianity.* London, Hodder and Stoughton, 1911.

Wright, C. J., *Miracle in History and in Modern Thought.* New York, Holt, Rinehart and Winston, Inc., 1930.

SOURCES

Page	Line	

Page	Line	
14	17	Mark 6:34, RSV.
14	20	Matthew 14:14, RSV.
14	29	Mark 6:36, RSV.
15	1	Mark 6:37, RSV.
15	31	The equivalent of $40 then; $60 in value now.
16	22	John 6:9, RSV.
17	5	Luke 9:14, RSV.
17	13	John 6:11, RSV.
17	23	John 6:12, RSV.
19	13	John 6:15, RSV.
19	19	John 6:26, NEB.
19	24	John 6:35, KJV.
19	29	John 6:27, KJV.
19	34	John 6:34, RSV.
20	11	Trench, *op. cit.*, p. 386.
20	21	Mark 8:3, RSV.

CHAPTER 3

24	30	Matthew 14:23, RSV.
25	12	Mark 6:47-48, NEB.
25	18	John 15:5, KJV.

CHAPTER 4

31	13	Mark 3:21, NEB.
35	3	Katharina von Schlegel.

CHAPTER 5

37	15	Luke 13:6-9, KJV.
38	13	Trench, *op. cit.*, p. 474.
38	16	Mark 11:12, NEB.
38	28	Mark 11:14, NEB.
40	19	T. S. Eliot, "The Hippopotamus," *Collected Poems, 1909-1962* (Harcourt, Brace & World, Inc.)
41	28	Mark 11:21, NEB.
41	34	Mark 11:22-24, NEB.

CHAPTER 6

45	4	Matthew 17:24, NEB.
46	14	Matthew 5:17, KJV.
46	15	Luke 4:16, KJV.
46	27	Matthew 17:25-26, NEB.
47	9	Matthew 17:27, NEB.
47	22	Trench, *op. cit.*, pp. 417-418.

CHAPTER 7

52	18	I am indebted for this wisdom to Dr. John Lamy, minister emeritus, College Hill Presbyterian Church, Cincinnati, Ohio.
52	25	Luke 5:5, NEB.
53	6	Psalms 127:1, KJV.
53	15	Luke 5:5, NEB.
53	16	Luke 5:6-7, NEB.
53	25	Psalms 8:6-8, KJV.
54	14	Exodus 20:19, KJV.
54	16	Trench, *op. cit.*, p. 142.
54	26	Luke 5:10, NEB.
55	8	Sermon CCCLXXXI.
56	12	Luke 5:11, NEB.
56	33	Trench, *op. cit.*, p. 150.
57	18	John 21:3-4, NEB.
57	19	John 21:5, NEB.
57	22	John 21:6, NEB.
57	28	John 21:6-7, NEB.
57	34	John 21:9-13, NEB.
58	25	John 21:15, NEB.
58	31	John 21:18, NEB.

CHAPTER 8

65	11	Leslie Weatherhead, *Psychology, Religion, and Healing* (Abingdon Press), p. 39.
66	1	*Ibid.*, p. 38.
66	6	Healings in the Old Testament were isolated exceptions to the rule.
66	7	Weatherhead, *op. cit.*, p. 38.
66	10	*Ibid.*
66	12	Jesus healed seven patients on the sabbath. The four not taken up in this chapter are: the man born blind (John 9:1-14), Legion (Mark 1:21-27), the hunchback (Luke 13:10-17), and Peter's mother-in-law (Mark 1:29-31).
67	2	Mark 2:27, KJV.
67	21	Matthew 12:9-10, NEB.
67	22	"The man probably had an atrophied hand or arm" (Sherman E. Johnson, *The Interpreter's Bible*, vol. 7, Abingdon Press, p. 394).
67	30	Mark 3:4, RSV.

Page	Line	

CHAPTER 10

83	1	Luke 4:38, NEB.
83	17	Mark 1:29, KJV.
84	9	Luke 4:18, KJV.
84	12	Luke 4:23-30, RSV.
84	21	Luke 4:31, RSV.
84	34	Luke 4:38, NEB.
86	19	Johnson, *op. cit.*, p. 342.
86	22	Luke 4:37, NEB.
87	8	S. MacLean Gilmour, *The Interpreter's Bible*, vol. 8, p. 161.
87	28	Matthew 9:20-21, KJV.
87	31	Gilmour, *loc. cit.*
89	21	Trench, *op. cit.*, p. 205.

CHAPTER 11

96	1	"On His Blindness."
96	13	Matthew 9:28, NEB.
96	15	Mark 8:22, NEB.
96	28	Matthew 9:31, NEB.
97	9	Mark 8:24-25, NEB.
98	14	Luke 18:43, RSV.
98	28	John 9:4, NEB.
99	1	Trench, *op. cit.*, p. 316.
99	6	John 9:9, NEB.
99	19	John 9:9, NEB.
99	32	John 9:24, NEB.
100	5	John 9:25, NEB.
100	8	John 9:27, NEB.
100	10	John 9:29, NEB.
100	12	John 9:30-33, NEB.
100	19	John 9:34, NEB.
100	26	John 9:40-41, NEB.

CHAPTER 12

103	2	Matthew 15:30, RSV.
103	7	Mark 7:32, NEB.
103	11	Mark 7:33, NEB.
104	25	Mark 7:33, NEB.
105	3	Mark 7:37, NEB.
105	16	Gilmour, *op. cit.*, p. 391.
106	3	Matthew 26:53, RSV.

138 19 Mark 7:26, RSV.

139 8 *The Iliad.*

139 10 Matthew 15:24, RSV.

139 16 Matthew 15:26, RSV.

139 28 Matthew 15:27, RSV.

139 32 Matthew 15:28, RSV.

140 1 Trench, *op. cit.*, pp. 375-376.

140 32 Matthew 15:29, RSV.

CHAPTER 17

143 20 Mark 5:1, NEB.

144 3 It is important to note that although this incident is still called "The Story of the Gadarene Demoniac," Gadara is twenty-five miles from the lake and cannot have been the scene of the incident. We can hardly imagine two thousand pigs traveling twenty-five miles, crossing a wide and deep river called "the Yarmuk," and then throwing themselves into the sea! Mark speaks of "the country of the Gerasenes," but Gerasa is still farther away. It is the modern Jerash, which is thirty miles from the lake.

"The late Mr. T. R. Maltby suggests that Peter, speaking Aramaic with a Galilean accent, used to talk about Ger'sa, and that Mark, spelling it out in Greek letters, called the people Gerasenes, and was supposed by critics to have made a mistake, when he was only reporting with his usual accuracy. The village called Khersa, just behind the bluff to which I have referred, is undoubtedly the place indicated, for here we have the only spot on the whole shore of the lake where steep ground falls into deep water" (Weatherhead, *op. cit.*, p. 54).

144 4 *Ibid.*, pp. 53-54.

144 21 Mark 5:1, NEB.

144 22 Matthew 8:28, RSV.

144 23 Mark 5:3-6, NEB.

145 3 Mark 5:7-9, NEB.

145 11 Romans 8:39, NEB.

145 17 Mark 5:9, NEB.

145 19 Weatherhead, *op. cit.*, p. 55.

145 32 Mark 5:9, NEB.

145 33 Gilmour, *op. cit.*, p. 158.